GLORIOUS FREEDOM

Glorious Freedom

The Excellency of the Gospel above the Law

RICHARD SIBBES

THE BANNER OF TRUTH TRUST

THE BANNER OF TRUTH TRUST
3 Murrayfield Road, Edinburgh EH12 6EL
P.O. Box 621, Carlisle, Pennsylvania 17013, USA

★

'Glorious Freedom' first published in 1639
© Banner of Truth 2000
ISBN 0 85151 791 9

Typeset in 10½/12pt Linotype Plantin
at The Spartan Press Ltd,
Lymington, Hants
Printed and bound in Great Britain by
Creative Print and Design (Wales),
Ebbw Vale

CONTENTS

Now the Lord is that Spirit: and where the Spirit of the Lord is, there is liberty.
But we all, with open face beholding as in a glass the glory of the Lord, are changed into the same image from glory to glory, even as by the Spirit of the Lord.

2 Corinthians 3:17–18

PUBLISHERS' PREFACE

The first edition of this work, entitled 'The Excellency of the Gospel above the Law', was published in 1639, four years after Sibbes' death. In the words of its editors, Thomas Goodwin and Philip Nye, it shows 'the liberty of the sons of God . . . the image of their graces here and glory hereafter'. Also, it provides 'much comfort and great encouragement to all [who] begin timely and continue constantly in the ways of God'.

Sibbes examines the fuller self-revelation of God in the coming of Christ and its greater effect in those who behold it by the Spirit. The vitality of the new covenant brings about spiritual liberty and likeness to Christ.

The original treatise is reproduced here with Goodwin's annotations incorporated and the language updated for clarity and ease of reading. It is also important to note here that Sibbes used both 'Spirit' and 'spirit' in a variety of ways. Because of the ambiguity of the word itself as well as the varying contexts in which it appears, the publishers have remained faithful to the author's original intent by reproducing these without alteration.

The same is true when speaking of the Holy Spirit. Though the full personhood of the Holy Ghost, or Holy Spirit, is unambiguously affirmed, both 'he' and 'it' are used in different grammatical contexts. These instances, too, are left unaltered.

The fuller edition of *Glorious Freedom* can be found in Volume 4 of *The Works of Richard Sibbes*.

The apostle begins this chapter with a commendation of his ministry, having been put upon it by the Corinthians' undervaluing him. Yet together with himself, he commends the Corinthians themselves as his best and only testimonial and letters of commendation (verse 2). In doing so, he makes way for himself to give a larger commendation of the glorious gospel itself, of which God 'hath made him so able a minister to them' (verse 6). And because the excellency of anything is best commended by comparing it with something else that excels in itself and yet is exceeded by it, he carries his commendation of the ministry of the gospel through the whole chapter by comparing it with the law and the ministry of the Old Testament.

The apostle makes this comparison firstly, by laying down a few distinct properties of the gospel in which it excels the law (verse 6):

- This was 'the ministry of the *New* Testament'; that of the law was of the Old.
- It was 'not of the letter', as the law was; 'but of the Spirit'.
- It was not of death, 'for the letter killeth'; but of life, for 'the Spirit quickeneth'.

Then, from these properties, he draws inferences which further illustrate the transcendent glory of the gospel.

THERE IS A GREATER GLORY IN THE NEW TESTAMENT

If only a ministration of the letter written and engraved in stone was glorious (verse 7); that is, if the literal notions and bare knowledge of the law, which (like dead words or characters) make no alteration at all, but leave their hearts hard and stony like the tables on which the law was written, which remained stones still; if even the literal knowledge of the law was glorious – as it was, both in the Jews' own account of themselves and in the judgement of the nations amongst whom they lived – 'how shall not the ministration of the Spirit be rather glorious?' (verse 8).

The meaning of this is largely explained in verse 3, where the Corinthians are said to be an 'epistle written not with ink' (or dead letters), 'but with the Spirit of the living God'. This kind of writing does not leave the heart a heart of stone, as the dead writing of the law did, but changes it into a 'heart of flesh' and thoroughly alters the whole man, as the writing within, ' in the tables of their hearts', is 'known and read of all men' (verse 2). So, with their lives corresponding to that spiritual and gracious writing of Christ in their hearts, they are 'manifestly declared to be the epistle of Christ'. By this ministry (and not by the law, [*Gal.* 3:2]), the Spirit of the living God is received, a Spirit of glory working glorious things both in the hearts and lives of men. Such a ministry as this is must therefore be 'rather [i.e. more] glorious'.

IT JUSTIFIES

We have another inference in verse 9: 'If the ministration of condemnation be glorious'; that is, if that word which 'concluded men under sin' (*Gal.* 3:22) and

[2]

pronounced the sentence of death upon them 'be glorious, much more does the ministration of righteousness exceed in glory'. For it is more glorious to pardon than to condemn; to give life, than to destroy. It is the glory of a man to pass over an offence (*Prov.* 19:11), and in God it is called the 'riches of his glory' (*Rom.* 9:23).

'The law, which was made glorious' in terrifying, condemning, and stopping the mouths of men, inasmuch as they had not a word to say for themselves, 'hath no glory, by reason of the glory' of the gospel 'that excelleth', in this very respect: it brings righteousness by its merit and the satisfaction given by it, so that we are justified and have peace towards God, notwithstanding the utmost rigour of the law.

IT REMAINS

The apostle argues further (verse 11): 'If that which is done away was glorious,' – as is the old covenant, which by the coming of the new was made old (*Heb.* 8:8) and removed as a thing grown weak and shaken (*Heb.* 12:27) – 'much more that which remaineth'. This is the new covenant, which cannot be shaken but shall remain, and is 'the everlasting gospel' (*Rev.* 14:6). It 'is more glorious', as God's last works exceed the former and, by comparison, take away the remembrance of them; as when he creates 'new heavens and a new earth', and the former shall not be remembered nor come to mind (*Isa.* 65:17).

ITS MESSAGE AND MINISTRY ARE CLEARER AND MORE COMFORTING

There is another excellency of the gospel above the law, which the apostle adds and insists upon more than all the rest: that is the comforting plainness and perspicuity of the doctrine and ministry of it. 'Seeing we have such hope, we use great plainness of speech' (verse 12). In this it excels the ministry of Moses in three ways (verses 13–15).

The content of Moses' ministry was terrifying, bringing shame, confusion of face, and condemnation to the hearers, who could not stand before him or steadfastly behold his face, such a dazzling and amazing light shined in his ministry.

Its expressions were obscure and dark, so 'the children of Israel could not see to the end of that which is abolished'; that is, they could not see the drift and scope of his ministry by reason of the types and shadows, which was 'the veil he put upon his face'.

Their minds were blinded. There was 'a veil upon their hearts', which is evident to this day in the experience of the Jews, who so cleave in their affection to Moses and to the shadows and ceremonies of his ministry, that they reject the scope and end of it, Jesus Christ crucified.

And they can do no other. For although the veil upon Moses' face is removed by the doctrine of the gospel, which shows us in all possible plainness the meaning of Moses in all those types and ceremonies; yet until the gospel in its spirit and efficacy comes home to their hearts and removes 'the veil that is upon their hearts' – that is, until their natural blindness and obstinacy are taken away – the Jews will unavoidably abide in their ignorance and bondage. The law cannot remove their blindness, but rather increases it, 'for although Moses be read, yet until this day remaineth the same veil untaken away' (verse 14).

Now, in opposition to law in its darkness and obscurity, the apostle exalts the gospel in that it is plain

[4]

and full of demonstration, and that the light of it is not terrifying and overwhelming, but sweet and comforting. We may therefore, with much liberty and boldness of spirit, look constantly upon the great and glorious things set before us in it, although it is no other but the glory of the Lord Jesus Christ.

IT TRANSFORMS INWARDLY

And there is, moreover, such an efficacy and working power in this ministry of the gospel that it will not allow men to remain without alteration, as they did under Moses' ministry, though he was read daily. But it will 'change' them even 'into the image of Jesus Christ' and carry them on still in that image and likeness, from 'one degree of glory to another', by a most admirable and spiritual manner of working.

This special excellency and prerogative of the gospel is laid down in the last two verses of this chapter, which we shall now discuss more fully.

2: *The Spirit of Christ*

'Now the Lord is that Spirit: and where the Spirit of the Lord is, there is liberty.'

Here the apostle sets down what Christ is by what he does and its sweet effect: Christ is 'that Spirit' because he gives the Spirit; and 'where the Spirit of Christ is, there is liberty'.

CHRIST IS 'THAT SPIRIT'

The Spirit here is not to be taken for the person of God, as if the Holy Ghost had said, 'The Lord is a Spirit and not a bodily thing,' though that is true. Neither does it refer to the third person of the Godhead, as if Christ were the Holy Ghost. That would be a confusion of persons. Nor is it to be restricted to the third person, as if it meant the Holy Ghost is the Spirit. Nor, as some have argued, does it show that the Spirit is Jehovah, God. The expression 'The Lord is that Spirit' is neither to show that Christ is God, nor that the Spirit is God, nor that Christ is the Holy Ghost. But it is meant in regard of a special dispensation. That is, the Lord Jesus Christ, who is the Lord of his church by marriage and office and so on, 'is that Spirit'. That is, he has the Spirit in himself and gives the Spirit to others.

He has the Spirit eminently in himself, as man.
The Holy Ghost filled his human nature and made it

[6]

spiritual. The Spirit is all in all in the human nature of Christ; and whatever he does, he does, as it were, full of the Spirit in himself. He gives the Spirit as God, and receives him as man. So he both gives and receives. The Spirit proceeds from the Father and the Son as God, but the Spirit sanctified Christ as man, as in the virgin's womb. The Holy Ghost sanctified that blessed mass of his body and filled him with all graces and gifts. And so it is said, he received the Spirit without measure (*John* 3:34), that is, in abundance. Christ has the Spirit in himself in a more eminent and excellent manner than all others, and it must be so for these reasons:

a) From the near union between the human nature and the divine. They are one person. Therefore there is more Spirit in Christ than in all creatures put together; more than in all the angels and all men, because the divine nature is nearer to Christ than it is to the angels or to any creature.

b) Christ has the Spirit without measure, intensively and extensively. He has all graces in all degrees, even next to infinitely. All others have it in their measure and proportion.

c) The Spirit rests upon Christ without variation. In other men the Spirit ebbs and flows; sometimes more and sometimes less. There are spiritual desertions not only in regard of comfort, but in regard of grace, though not totally. But the Spirit rests on Christ eternally in full measure; and therefore it is said in Isaiah 11:2: 'The Spirit of the Lord shall rest upon him, the Spirit of wisdom and understanding, the Spirit of counsel and might,' and so on.

d) By reason of his offices in relation to the church. He is its head, husband, king, priest, prophet, and so on. The head is made by nature the seat of the more noble faculties, of seeing, hearing, understanding, and judging,

[7]

and is furnished accordingly with greater capacity for ruling and governing the whole body. So Christ is the head of the church, and the government of all the world is laid upon him, and all excellencies are derived from him to all his members, as life from the root is communicated to all the branches.

And therefore he must have the Spirit in greatest abundance. His fullness of the Spirit is as the fullness of the fountain; ours is but as the fullness of the cistern. He has grace in the spring; we have it but in the conduit. His graces are primary; ours derivative. We have nothing but what we have received. Therefore it is said, he has the oil of gladness poured upon him above his fellows (*Psa.* 45:7).

He has the name of 'Christ' by virtue of anointing. He was separated and ordained to the office of mediatorship by anointing, not literally with any material oil, but with the Spirit. This was in regard to his human nature only, but it was above his fellows; that is, above all kings and priests, for they are his fellows in regard to titles. He was above them all, for all have their anointing from him. Therefore he is the King of kings and the Prophet of prophets and so on, and also above all his fellows. We take his fellows to be Christians; 'I go to my God and your God' (*John* 20:17). He is the 'first-born' amongst them, and in all things he has the pre-eminence.

e) He is to be the pattern, and we are to follow him. We are predestined to be conformed to him (*Rom.* 8:29) and to grow up to that fullness which is in him. And in this respect, he has the Spirit and all graces in greater abundance that he might exceed all, even Christians of greatest growth and perfection. He is to be a pattern and example to all, the strongest as well as the weak. Even Paul himself, who was a leader to others, for the excellency of the grace of Christ that was in him, was yet a follower of Christ. 'Be you followers of me, as I am of Christ' (*1 Cor.* 11:1).

Question. When did this fullness of the Spirit come upon Christ? When did he have it?

Answer 1. A fullness of the Spirit was poured out upon Christ in the union of the human nature with the divine. Union and unction went together. There was an anointing of the Spirit together with the union of the Spirit.

Answer 2. There was a fuller manifestation of the Spirit in his baptism. When the Holy Ghost fell on him in the shape of a dove, he received the Spirit. He was to enter into the ministry of the gospel. 'The Spirit of the Lord God was upon him' because he had anointed him to preach good tidings unto the meek, and so on (*Isa.* 61:1).

Answer 3. But the fullest degree of declaration and manifestation of the Spirit upon Christ was after his resurrection, after he had satisfied fully for our salvation. Then the stop of his glory was taken away. For to work our salvation the glory of Christ was kept back from his human nature, that he might be abased to suffer for us. When he had fully suffered for us, that stay of his glory, his abasement, was taken away, and then nothing appeared but all glory and Spirit in Christ. All things were put under his feet, and he was set upon his throne as a glorious king. His prophetic office appeared before his death, his priestly office appeared in his death. But then in the resurrection he appeared as king and Lord of all.

Thus we see how Christ is that Spirit; that is, he is full of the Spirit in regard of himself.

He is 'that Spirit' of all truths and of all persons, giving them life.
What is the scope of all the Scriptures but Christ – from the first promise of the blessed seed, The seed of the

woman shall break the serpent's head (*Gen.* 3:15), to the end of the Bible? What are all the Scriptures without Christ? The law is a dead letter; and indeed, so is the gospel without Christ. He is 'that Spirit' which gives life to all the Scriptures. Moses without Christ is but a shadow without a body, or a body without a soul. Take away Christ, what was the brazen serpent? What was the ark? What were the sacrifices? What is all? Is not Christ 'all in all' in these? The kings and priests and prophets, they were types of Christ; all the promises were made and fulfilled in Christ. The ceremonial law aimed at Christ, and the moral law is to drive us to Christ. Christ is the Spirit of all. And the Scripture without Christ is but a mere dead thing, a shell without a kernel, as it is to the Jews to this day.

He gives life to all people. He is a universal principle of spiritual life, infusing it into all his church and children. Christ has always been with his church from the beginning of the world, and will be to the end. It was no loss to the church that Christ in his bodily presence left it, for he left it 'the Comforter', his Spirit, and greater works were wrought after his ascension than before. He is 'anointed with the oil of gladness' and grace 'above his fellows' (*Psa.* 45:7), but all was for his fellows. Whatever he is or has, all is for his church and children. 'For us' he was born, 'for us' he was given. He is a king, a priest, a prophet for us. He died for us, he rose again for us.

And all that he does towards the church, he does as the one who has the Spirit, and he does it by the Spirit. The Father is the first in the Trinity, '*from* whom' all comes; and the Son, '*by* whom' all things are; but the Holy Ghost is the immediate worker of all things, nearest to the creature. All things are applied *from* God the Father, *through* the Son, *by* the Spirit. What Christ wrought, and what the Father in wisdom devised, was applied by the Spirit; and so also by the Spirit we are made fit for such a glorious condition as we have by Christ. And this is why Christ gives the Spirit to those to whom he purposes to give faith or love, or to work any gracious work.

For where Christ saves, he does it not only by merit and satisfying the wrath of God for us, but also by sanctifying and working effectually in us, that he might be a perfect Saviour. Now the essential vigour and operative principle in all things, wrought either by the Father or from the Son, is the Spirit. As in man, who resolves and purposes from his will, proceeds from his wisdom and understanding, and then executes and does all by vigorous power, so it is in this working of God. The Father devises and determines what to do; the Son, who is the wisdom of the Father (*1 Cor.* 1:24), dispenses what the Father wills; the Holy Spirit, the power of both, finishes and works all upon us, and therefore he is called the 'power of the highest' (*Luke* 1:35).

Whatever works come from God to creatures in general as works of creation and providence are done immediately by the Holy Spirit as the third person coming from the Father and the Son. But in those special works wrought in his church and on his children, all things come from the Holy Ghost, not simply as the third person, but as 'the Spirit of Christ' – that is, first sanctifying and filling the human nature of Christ, and then sanctifying and filling us. Christ could not give the Holy Ghost immediately to us, as we are at enmity with God and separated from him through our sins. He must first take the Spirit to himself and, having by his death and sufferings reconciled us to his Father and purchased the Spirit *for* us, he may now give his Spirit *to* us.

If we had stood in Adam, we would not have received

grace as we do now. We would have received it from the first Adam as from only a man. Now we receive it not from mere man, but, much more, from the 'second Adam', who is God-man. Indeed, Adam himself did not receive his grace in so glorious a manner as we do, for he received it from the Spirit only as the third person in the Trinity and as all other creatures received their excellencies. But we receive it from the Holy Spirit, which not only proceeds from the Father and the Son, but comes to us, as it were, through our own nature, which was marvellously united to God the Son and made one with him – and having come to us, works in us.

'The first Adam was made a living soul; the last Adam was made a quickening Spirit' (*1 Cor.* 15:45). He quickened himself when he was dead, and he quickens all his members, too. First he receives the Spirit himself, and the same Spirit that filled and sanctified his human nature also sanctifies his church, which he 'loves even as himself'. As he loves his own human nature, which the Holy Ghost sanctified, so he loves his own mystical body, his church, which is mystically united to him, and he sanctifies it by the same Spirit. Christ, as head of his church, dispenses his Spirit to us, in various respects:

(a) As he is God, by way of *immediate influence*. He pours the Spirit out upon us as the prime and principal cause. And this he does as God, not as man, for manhood cannot work above itself, cannot do the work of God, cannot work grace or give the Spirit.

(b) As he is man, joined together with the Godhead, by way of *merit and satisfaction*. He procures the Spirit to be given and poured out, which is done by the Father and the Son on all those who are beloved in the Son. The Spirit is given by Christ, with the Father, as mediator, meritoriously. For he by suffering and satisfying procured the gift. Christ himself is the first gift, indeed, the greatest that was ever given, the giving of Christ to die to satisfy the wrath of God and obtain eternal life. Next to that main gift is the gift of the Spirit, in which is the seed of all gifts and graces; and this we have by his merit and mediatorship. Yet we must also remember that although Christ is said to give the Spirit, as he does, yet the Holy Spirit gives himself, too. For there is such a unity of consent and nature in the Trinity, that though the Father and the Son send the Spirit, yet the Spirit comes of his own self.

(c) We have the Spirit from Christ not only by merit, but also by *example*. He is the exemplary cause of all graces in us. Looking to him we are transformed, as we shall see, 'from glory to glory'. For when we consider how much Christ has done for us as to save us, and redeem us, and die for us, this brings forth in us a love for Christ and makes us think of him often and desire to imitate him, as we usually do those we love and highly esteem.

(d) The dispensation of the Spirit is most abundant *after the resurrection of Christ*. He appeared in himself to be most spiritual and glorious after he rose again; so being as the sun in its full height and perfect beauty, he casts his beams most plentifully abroad, because:

Having finished the work of redemption and satisfied the justice and wrath of God fully, there was nothing to hinder the blessed gift of the Spirit. It is said that before, the Holy Ghost had not been given because Christ had not been glorified (*John* 7:39). The gift of the Holy Ghost especially depends upon the glorifying of Christ. When he had fulfilled the work of redemption and was raised to glory, God, being pacified, gave the Holy Ghost as a gift of his favour.

Having risen and ascended, he is now in heaven. He therefore gave the Holy Ghost more abundantly than before to his church, because he has the advantage of being exalted on high – just as that glorious creature the sun, by its advantage in being placed in the heavens above, can shine upon the greatest part of the earth at all times, and we do not need to call the sun down from its place to come into our houses or fields or gardens; no. Where it is seated in its proper place, it is in the very best position to send down heat and light and influence to lower things.

So, Christ does his church more good now that he is in heaven, from where he sends the Spirit, than he could do if he were below, because though his human nature is confined in heaven, his person is everywhere. And being 'ascended now far above all heavens', he gives gifts more liberally and plentifully, inasmuch as he fills all things (*Eph.* 4:10). He enlarges the tents of his gospel and has taken in a greater people to himself. We see in winter, when the sun is low and near the earth, all things are dead and cold; but when the sun in spring comes to a higher point above us, all things put on new garments. There is a new vigour and freshness in them.

So there was more abundant vigour of the Spirit when Christ came in the flesh; his virtue appeared much more in every way than before. But when this blessed Son of righteousness was advanced and seated at the right hand of his Father, where his nature was perfectly enriched and perfectly adorned with all kinds of graces in their highest glory, and with his influence of light and heat now increasing and its efficacy and working to be felt everywhere, the glorious beams of the sun began to be scattered and the light of the gospel to shine to a greater number of people. Now there was no respect of persons, whether Jew or Gentile, bond or free, male or female; all was one. The commission was enlarged to all: 'Go, preach the gospel to every creature' (*Mark* 16:15); and with the Word the Spirit went and was received; and many thousands were 'added to the church', even those as 'should be saved' (*Acts* 2:47).

We have opened the meaning of the words and shown how 'Christ is that Spirit': that the Spirit is eminently in him, and that he gives the Spirit and gives gifts by the Spirit. All the spiritual and supernatural vigour and life and influence we have is from the Spirit; and whatever the Spirit has or does for us is done as sent from Christ, in whom the Spirit is in all fullness. Now we will show how these truths will be profitable and useful to us in the course of our lives and for the comfort of our spirits.

Use 1. Christ is the Spirit of the Scriptures, of all truths, of all ordinances.
We can therefore reconcile scriptures with one another when they seem to contradict. The law is said to be a dead letter, a 'ministration of condemnation' (*2 Cor.* 3:6,9), but in Psalm 19:7 it is said, 'The law of the Lord is perfect, converting the soul.' These texts are reconciled in this way: the law is said to be dead, and so it is, without Christ, without the Spirit who gives life; and the gospel, too, is 'a savour of death' (*2 Cor.* 2:16). The sacraments also, as well as the Word, are dead ordinances if Christ is not in them. But the law is said to be 'perfect' and 'to convert the soul' when the Spirit goes along with it, as before Christ came in the flesh, as in David's time. But after the coming of Christ, who was the substance of those shadows, they became 'beggarly elements', as in Paul's time (*Gal.* 4:9). And the Spirit worked not with them, but with the gospel, 'the hearing of faith' (*Gal.* 3:2).

[15]

We can also understand why we obtain more comfort at one time than another from an ordinance (be it Word or sacrament), and why it benefits one person and not another. This is from the presence or absence of Christ, who is 'that Spirit'. Why does wine refresh and strengthen more than common water? It is of the same substance and colour as water. But there is more spirit in it. All things work according to the spirits in them. So why does the reading or hearing of the same thing affect one, and another not at all? The substance of the thing is the same, but the Spirit is not the same. The Spirit goes with one, and not with the other. We grant that our negligence in preparation and attention, our pride and earthly-mindedness, our lack of faith to mingle with the Word – these or the like may cause us many times to be sent away empty. Yet it still must be observed as a most evident truth that all the efficacy and fruit of any ordinance depend upon the presence in it of Christ, who is 'that Spirit' that quickens.

The most powerful means that ever was ordained for our good will be dead and heartless if he is not there by his Spirit to put life into it. It may seem strange what John says, 'The flesh profiteth nothing' (*John* 6:63). The flesh of Christ – our nature which Christ took and in which so much was wrought for us, which is the greatest ordinance of all – yet this flesh 'profiteth not', nor will there be any benefit from it, if it is not applied to us spiritually. For it is not the flesh itself, but by it and with it that we receive the Spirit of Christ, the Spirit who quickens and makes the flesh of Christ to be 'meat indeed'. And as it is with the flesh of Christ, so with all other ordinances. The Scriptures profit nothing, preaching profits nothing, the sacraments profit nothing; none of these will be 'meat indeed' unless the Spirit of Christ quickens them.

We should therefore desire that Christ would join his Spirit to all the ordinances of God and make them effectual. We ought to come to the ordinances in dependence upon Christ, who is the life and scope of all, for a blessing upon them and for his presence in them; and then we would not find such dullness and deadness in them. It is the sin of this age, this formality. It is the sin of those that have anything in them. Set desperate drunkards and other such wretches aside, those who plainly find themselves activated by the spirit of the devil. But take those who conform in any fashion to religion, and the killing sin that they lie under is this dead formality. They will hear a sermon now and then, look at a book, and perhaps pray morning and evening, but never look up to the living and quickening Spirit, Jesus Christ. So all they do is dead and loathsome, like salt that has no savour. What is the best liquor if it has lost its life and spirit, but flat and unsavoury? And blood when the spirits are out of it, what is it but loathsome gore? So are all their performances like sacrifices that had no fire in them. The Lord loathed such sacrifices as he did Cain's; and he loathes all our flat and lifeless services and, indeed, our persons too, being fleshly and 'not having the Spirit' (*Jude* 19).

What need there is to sanctify all we take in hand by prayer! When we go to hear a sermon, when we take up the Bible to read a chapter, alone or in our families, we should lift up our eyes and hearts and voices to heaven; we should say to Christ, 'Lord, join thy Spirit, be present with us. Without thee thy Word is dead; our hearts are dead and will harden under the means and darken in the light, and we shall fall under the heavy condemnation of these secure and formal times, if thou leavest us.'

[17]

Use 2. Christ is said to be 'that Spirit', to send the Spirit as God, and to receive him as man, in fullness, for our sakes.

It is a point of much comfort that there is such abundance of Spirit in our nature in Christ, and for the benefit of the church, that we have a fullness from which to receive. It was a comfort to Joseph's brothers and that family that Joseph was full of honour, ruling as the second in the kingdom. Therefore they lacked nothing that was good in Egypt. Is it not a comfort for Christians to know that Christ is the Spirit – that he has the Spirit to give, the Spirit of wisdom in all difficulties, the Spirit of truth to keep us from all errors, the Spirit of strength for all services, the Spirit of comfort for all afflictions? He who is their Lord has abundance of Spirit in him, and for them.

Therefore, when we want any grace, or gift of the Spirit, we should go to Christ; for God does all by Christ, and Christ does all by the Spirit. Desire Christ, that he would grant his Spirit to rule us, counsel us, comfort us, and strengthen us. In our emptiness, as indeed we are empty creatures of ourselves, let us go to Christ for the Spirit. He has received that fullness for us; desire of him that out of his fullness he would vouchsafe to give to us.

The reason Christians are so dead and dull and dark in their spirits is that they do not first consider themselves, and then go to Christ. We should all, in all necessities whatever, make use of this our great high treasurer, the great high steward of heaven and earth; of this our Joseph, the second person in heaven. He is at the right hand of God, and all to fill his church with his Spirit. Our comfort is now that our strength and comfort lie hidden in Christ who, as man, is near to us, and as God, is near to God. He is between the Father and us; he is near the Father, being of the same nature with him; he is near us, being of the same nature with us. So being a mediator in office, and being so fit to be a mediator in nature, what a comfort this is.

Indeed, there is no coming to God, no interaction between God and us directly, but only through the God-man, who is the mediator between God and us. In Christ we go to God, in our flesh, in our nature; and in Christ, and from Christ, and by Christ, we have all grace and comfort. From Christ as God, together with the Holy Ghost and the Father, we have all; and we have all in Christ as a head and husband; and we have all through Christ as mediator by his merit. Therefore we should go to Christ in every way.

Use 3. Let us labour to be in Christ that we may get the Spirit.
It is greatly necessary that we should have the Spirit. Above all things, next to redemption by Christ, labour for the Spirit of Christ. Christ is our Saviour not only by merit and satisfaction, but by efficacy and grace; that is, as he has purchased us for his people by his blood, so he will subdue our corruptions and rule us by his Spirit.

Any man that has not the Spirit of Christ 'is none of his' (*Rom.* 8:9). Those that do not have the efficacy of the Spirit in them to rule them shall not have benefit by his death to reconcile them, for these always go together: Christ as a king to rule and as a priest to die. He 'came by water and blood' (*1 John* 5:6) to satisfy and to sanctify.

There is a necessity of the Spirit that we be new creatures. It was the Spirit's brooding upon the chaos that brought everything forth (*Gen.* 1:2); so the Spirit must sit upon our souls before any change will be made. Now it is necessary for us to be changed and made new, or else we can never inhabit the new heavens and the new earth. We must have the Spirit of God. Therefore, as in the material temple, it is not by might, nor by power, but by the Spirit (*Zech.* 4:6); so in raising up spiritual temples it is not by physical or mental strength, but by the Spirit. Therefore the Spirit is necessary for us, just as our being in grace is necessary.

We know that, till the Spirit came more abundantly upon the holy apostles, what dark creatures they were! But when the Holy Ghost had come upon them, how full of life and light and courage they were – that the more they suffered, the more they might suffer! So it will be with Christians. The more spiritual they grow, the more full of light and courageous; the stronger, livelier and vigorous for all duties. The Holy Ghost is the substantial vigour of all creatures; all the spiritual strength of everything comes from the Holy Spirit, and the Holy Spirit from Christ.

For nothing can work above itself. Nature cannot work above nature. What elevates nature above itself, and sets a spiritual stamp, and puts divine qualities on it, is the Spirit of God. That divine quality is called spirit. There is the flesh and the spirit. All in us is flesh by nature; whatever is spiritual and divine comes from the Spirit, and so is called spirit. You see therefore the necessity of the working of the Spirit, just as it is necessary to be new creatures and to be spiritual. If we are to be spiritual, we must receive that quality from him who is first spiritual, the Spirit himself, the principle and fountain of all that is spiritual.

Let us labour to be in Christ also that we may serve and suffer in ways that exceed what human nature can bear. To do and suffer things that are above nature, we must have a spirit above nature: when we feel sin, to believe the forgiveness of sins; when we see death, to believe life everlasting; and when we are in extremity, to believe God present with us to deliver us. To believe contraries in contraries is a strange, almighty work of faith by the work of the Spirit. It is above the work of nature to die, to end our days with comfort, and to resign up our souls, for nature sees nothing but darkness and desolation and destruction in the grave. Nothing can make a man comfortable in death except that which raises him above nature, the Spirit of God.

Now if we are Christians we must do and suffer these things, and many others like them; and therefore we must have the Spirit to enable us to do them. The Spirit is to the soul as the soul is to the body. What is the body without the soul? A carcass, a loathsome dead thing. What is the soul without the Spirit? A chaos of darkness and confusion.

Use 4. How can we know whether or not we have the Spirit of Christ?

a) By the activity of the Spirit. The Spirit is a vigorous working being, and therefore all three persons take upon them the name of Spirit, but the Holy Ghost especially, because he is the spiritual vigour. The Spirit is an operative entity. The spirit is the pure essence of something, that is, nothing but operation. God, who is nothing but a pure act, is said to be a spirit. Those that have the Spirit of God are full of activity and energy. Shall the spirits of bodies be vigorous, and shall not the Holy Ghost be vigorous, who is a substantial vigour? Therefore, if a man has the Spirit of God in him, it will work in him; it is very operative.

The Spirit is compared to fire in several respects:

Fire is of a working nature. It is the instrument of

nature. If we did not have fire, what could we work? All materials and all things are worked by fire, especially metals; they are framed and made malleable by fire. The Holy Ghost, too, works to soften the heart and make us malleable, making us fit for the impression of all good.

Fire makes dark bodies light like itself. Iron is a dark body, but if the fire penetrates it, it makes it light. We are dark creatures of ourselves; if we have the Spirit it makes us light.

Fire makes cheerful and ascends upwards. If a man has the Spirit of God, his way of life will be upward and heavenly; his mind is on the things of God, and he does not grovel here below. So in different ways the Holy Ghost is compared to fire and has certain effects in us. In some way we find our understandings enlightened and ourselves quickened and carried up to the nature above, in holy and heavenly actions – and that is a good sign that we have the Spirit of Christ.

A part will follow the whole. We know that a clump of soil falls down because all the soil is heavy; when all the soil falls down, every little clod will fall with it. So Christ our head, who has abundance of the Spirit, is in heaven; and if we have the Spirit we will follow him, and attend to the things where Christ is.

b) By the conviction given by the Spirit. Where the Spirit of Christ is it also convinces (*John* 16:8). That is, it brings a clear evident conviction with it, that the truth of God *is* the truth of God. It is not doubtful. Therefore when a man staggers in the truth, whether he should do this or that, it is a sign he does not have the Spirit, or that he has it in a very small measure, because as light the Spirit is convincing. A man does not doubt what he sees at noonday. So what he sees by the Spirit he is convinced of. When a man doubts and wavers whether he should take a good course or a bad, it is a sign he is carnal and does not have the Spirit of God; for the Spirit would convince him. You must take *this* course if you will be saved. *That* is said to convince; and when the Spirit says something to convince, that says more for a thing than anything can say against it.

Now when a man has the Spirit of God, he can say more for God and for good things and good ways than all the devils in hell by discouragement can say against them. And, when a man cannot say anything for God and for good causes to purpose, he does not have the Spirit of God. The Spirit of God would so convince him that he would answer all cavillings and objections. The argument for this is wondrously full, and I have given you but a taste, to know whether or not the Spirit of Christ is in you.

c) By the Spirit's transforming us. In a word, if Christ is 'that Spirit' and has infused the Spirit into us, it will make us like him. It will transform us into his likeness, making us holy and humble and obedient as he was, even to death. This subject might be treated more fully, but we have occasion to speak on it in other portions of Scripture.

Use 5. That you may have the Spirit of God, take these directions.

a) We must *go to Christ, study Christ.* If we will have the Spirit, study the gospel of Christ. Why, before Christ, was there so little Spirit in comparison? Because there was but little measure of the knowledge of Christ. The more Christ is revealed, the more is the Spirit given. And according to the manifestation of Christ, what he has and has done for us, the more the riches of Christ are unfolded in the church, the more the Spirit goes along with them. The more the free grace and love of

God in Christ alone are made known to the church, the more Spirit there is – and the reverse is also true: the more Spirit, the more knowledge of Christ, for there is a reciprocal going of these two, the knowledge of Christ and the Spirit.

Why was there little of the Spirit in the clever and able schoolmen of popery? Because they did not savour the gospel. They were wondrously bright, but they did not savour the matters of grace and of Christ. It was not fully revealed to them, but they attributed it to satisfaction, and to merits, and to the pope, the head of the church, and so on. They divided Christ, they did not know him; and dividing Christ, they wanted the Spirit of Christ, and wanting that Spirit, they did not teach Christ as they should. Those were dark times, as they themselves confessed, especially about A.D. 900 to 1000, because Christ was veiled in a world of idle ceremonies – to darken the gospel and the victory of Christ – made by the pope, who was the vicar of Satan. These were the doctors of the church then, and Christ was hidden and wrapped in idle traditions and ceremonies of men; and that was the reason that things were obscure.

Now when Christ, and all good things by Christ and by him only, are revealed, the veil is taken off. Now for these past hundred years, in the time of reformation, there has been more Spirit and more light and comfort. Christians have lived and died more comforted. Why? Because Christ has been more known. And as it is with the church, so it is with individual Christians: the more they study Christ and the fullness that is in Christ, and all comfort to be had in him alone – 'wisdom, righteousness, sanctification, and redemption' (*1 Cor.* 1:30) – the more they grow spiritually. And the more spiritually they grow, the more they grow in the knowledge of Christ. Therefore, if we want to have the Spirit, let us come near to Christ and labour to know him more, who is the fountain of all that is spiritual.

b) If we would be spiritual, let us *take heed that we do not trust too much in dead things,* without Christ; having a kind of legalism in the work done, thinking that reading, and hearing, and receiving the sacrament, and the government of the church will do it – as if it were as man would have it. These are excellent things, but what are they without the Spirit of Christ? Though a man may hear ever so much and receive the sacrament ever so often, he may be dead with all these if he does not go to Christ, the quickening Spirit, in this manner: 'Lord, these, and my soul too, are dead things without thy Spirit; therefore quicken me.' Join Christ with all our performances, without which all is nothing, and then he will be spiritual to us.

c) And when we ask Christ for the Spirit – we must if we will have it, and God will give the Holy Ghost to those who ask him (*Luke* 11:13) – let us remember to *use the means carefully: reading, and hearing, and holy communion of saints.* Though these without the Spirit can do nothing, the Spirit is not given except by these. They are the golden conduits of the Spirit of Christ. No man is ever spiritual except by reading, hearing, conferring about good things and attending upon the means of salvation, because God works using his own tools and instruments. That is why it is said that John was 'in the Spirit on the Lord's day' (*Rev.* 1:10). Let a Christian sanctify the Sabbath as he should do, and he will be in the Spirit on the Lord's day more than on other days. Why? Because then he is reading, and hearing, and conferring, and thinking of spiritual matters; and the more a man on the Lord's day is in a

[25]

spiritual course, the more he is in the Spirit: John 'was in the Spirit on the Lord's day.'

With this we end our discussion of the words 'The Lord is that Spirit'.

3: *Liberty*

'Where the Spirit of the Lord is, there is liberty.'

We see from this what it is the Spirit works. Let us return to my previous example. We say the sun is heat and influence; that is not strictly so, for they are the products. But the sun appears to us to comfort by its heat and influence, and so that is what we say. We say of a man that he is all spirit. So Christ is all Spirit. The sun is all light, and where the light and heat of the sun are, there is fruitfulness. So Christ is all Spirit, and where the Spirit of Christ is, there is spiritual liberty.

It would be unnecessary to discuss different kinds of liberty. Everyone desires liberty, but we misunderstand the means of it, the way to attain it. Here we see where to obtain it, from the Spirit of Christ. Liberty is a sweet thing, especially liberty from the greatest enemies of all. Man's nature delights in liberty from tyranny and base servitude; he who does not abhor tyranny does not have the nature of a man. And if outward liberty is such a sweet thing, what shall we think then of the liberty of the Spirit from the great enemies that daunt the greatest monarchs in the world? Liberty from the anger of the great God; liberty from Satan, God's executioner; liberty from the terror of conscience, from the fear of death, and hell, and judgement – what shall we think of liberty in these respects? Indeed, we speak of great matters when we speak of liberty.

Now liberty is either Christian liberty or gospel liberty. You may think this a fine difference, but there is some reality in it. Christian liberty belongs to all, even to those before Christ. Though they do not have the term of Christians, they were members of Christ. Christ was head of the church 'yesterday, and today, and for ever' (*Heb.* 13:8). Gospel liberty is that which is more appropriated since the coming of Christ.

Now the liberty that belongs to Christians as Christians, spiritual and inward liberty, frees us from those grand enemies, the greatest enemies of all. Gospel liberty, besides that, frees also outwardly from the ceremonial and moral law and such like; and it frees from the restraint of the law. The Jews were under many restraints that now under the gospel we are not. I speak therefore of liberty as it runs through all ages, not only since the time of Christ. Where the Spirit is, both these liberties are, now since the coming of Christ.

CHRISTIAN LIBERTY

The words 'Where the Spirit of Christ is, there is liberty' imply that we are in bondage before we have the Spirit of Christ. And indeed that is true. For outside of Christ we are slaves, the best of us all are slaves. In Christ, the lowest of all is a free man and a king. Out of Christ there is nothing but thraldom. We are under the kingdom of the devil. When he calls us, we come. We are in thraldom under the wrath of God, under the fear of death and damnation, and all those spiritual enemies that I need not mention; they are known to you well enough by frequent experience. There is no man who is not a slave till he is in Christ; and the more free a man thinks himself to be, and labours to be, the more enslaved he is.

For take a man that labours to have his liberty, to do what he chooses. He thinks it the happiest condition in the world; others think the best condition is not to be tyrannized by others. It is the disposition of man's nature without grace. They consider it happiness to have their wills over all others, but the more liberty they have in this, the more slavery. Why?

The more liberty that a man has to do lawlessly what he will, contrary to justice and equity, the more he sins. The more he sins, the more he is enthralled to sin. The more he is enthralled to sin, the more he is in bondage to the devil and becomes the enemy of God. To pick out the most wretched man in the world, I would pick out the greatest man in the world, if he is wicked, who has the most people under him; he has most liberty, and seeks most liberty, and accounts it his happiness that he may have his liberty. This is the greatest thraldom of all, and it will prove so when he dies and comes to answer for it. Therefore the point does not need much proof, that if we are not in Christ we are slaves, as Augustine said in his book *The City of God*, 'He is a slave though he domineer and rule.'

A man till he is in Christ is a slave, not of one man or one lord over him, but he has as many lords as he has lusts. There are but two kingdoms that the Scripture speaks of, the kingdom of Satan and darkness, and the kingdom of Christ. All that are not in the kingdom of Christ, in that blessed liberty, must be in the other kingdom of Satan. This is basic. Therefore I mention it briefly as an incentive and provocation to stir us up, to get into Christ, to get the Spirit of Christ, that we may have this spiritual liberty; or else we are all slaves, notwithstanding all our civil liberties, whatever they be.

Now, 'where the Spirit of Christ is, there is liberty': freedom from that bondage that we are in by nature and which is strengthened by a wicked course of life. For though we are all born slaves by nature, by a wicked course of life we put ourselves into bonds and entangle ourselves. So many sins and so many repetitions of sin, so many cords – the longer a man lives the greater slave he is. Now when the Spirit of Christ comes, it frees us from all, from both natural and habitual slavery.

This liberty is wrought by Christ and applied by the Spirit. What Christ works he makes ours by his Spirit, which takes all from Christ. As Christ does all by the Spirit, so the Spirit takes all from Christ. All the comfort it has is from reasons taken from Christ, and foundations from Christ, and doctrines from Christ. Yet both have their efficacy – Christ as the meritorious cause, and the Spirit as the applying cause. The Spirit reveals the state of bondage we are in by nature, and reveals besides this a more excellent condition. And as it reveals, the Spirit of God brings us to this state by working faith in what Christ has done for us. Christ has freed us by his death from the curse of the law, from the wrath of God, from death and damnation. Now whatever Christ has done, the Spirit works faith in, to make this our own by uniting us to Christ. When Christ and we are one, his sufferings are ours, and his victory is ours, all is ours. Then, the Spirit persuading us of the love of God, and Christ redeeming us from that cursed slavery we were in, that Spirit works in us love and other graces. The dominion of sin is broken more and more, and we are set at liberty by the Spirit.

Liberty does not originate with the Spirit, but the grand redeemer is Christ. By paying the price to divine justice, he redeems us, and he alone. We are in bondage to the wrath of God under his justice, and so justice must be satisfied before we can be free. We are freed by a strong hand from bondage to Satan, God's executioner and jailer. Christ frees us by his Holy Spirit, working such graces in us as to make us see the loathsomeness of that bondage, and likewise working grace in us to be in love with that better condition which the Spirit discloses to us. So the Spirit brings us out of bondage by revelation and by power. All whom Christ frees by paying the price for their redemption, those he also frees by his Spirit, revealing to them their bondage as well as the blessed condition of freedom to which they are to be brought. And he perfects that freedom little by little, till he brings them to a glorious freedom in heaven.

There are many reasons that Christ gives his liberating Spirit to those he has redeemed by his death and satisfaction of God's justice. To name only a few:

a) To inform us. Christ saves in accordance with the nature of those saved. He saves us as reasonable persons, for he saves us that he may make us friends. He saves us as men and redeems us as men. He not only pays a price for us as if buying a thing that is dead, but further, he frees us so that we may understand to what and by whom we are freed, and what condition we are freed from. So there must be a Spirit joined with the work of Christ to thoroughly inform us, we being creatures fit to be informed.

b) To acquaint us as friends with all the favours and blessings that he has given us, because God intends to come into covenant with us, that we may be friends with him to our glory and happiness. He makes known to us what misery he brings us out of, what happiness he brings us into, and what our duty is. This is the work of the Spirit, to show us what he has done for us, that we may be friends.

c) To provide a basis for love to God. God saves us by way of love in the covenant of grace. He desires that we may love him again and maintain love. Now how can this happen, if the Spirit of God does not reveal what God in Christ has done for us? There must be the Spirit to show to the eye of the soul, and to tell us what Christ has done for us.

d) To fit us for heaven, for that glory that God intends for us in election. This must be altogether by the Spirit. The same Spirit that sanctified Christ in the womb, the same Spirit that anointed Christ, anoints all those that are Christ's, that they may be fit for so glorious a head. So there must be the Spirit as well as Christ in the work of redemption and liberty.

The Spirit of God sets us at liberty in the whole course and carrying out of salvation, from the beginning to the end, when he calls us, justifies us, sanctifies us and fully glorifies us.

a) He sets us at liberty first *in calling us powerfully and effectually.* Living in the church does not set us at liberty unless the Spirit stir us up to answer a divine call. 'For many are called, but few chosen' (*Matt.* 20:16). In the church there are Hagar and Ishmael as well as Isaac. There are hypocrites as well as sound Christians. There is outward baptism as well as inward. There is outward circumcision of the flesh as well as inward of the spirit. A man may have all these outward privileges and still be a slave in the very heart of the church; for Ishmael was a bond-slave though in the house of Abraham.

The beginning of spiritual liberty is when the Spirit of God in the ordinances, in the means of salvation, stirs up the heart to answer God's call. When we are exhorted to believe and repent, the Spirit gives power to respond to God, ' "Lord, I believe; help thou my unbelief" ' (*Mark* 9:24). Lord, I repent and desire to repent more and more.' When the Spirit of God in the ordinance says, 'Seek my face,' the soul replies, ' "Thy face, Lord, will I seek" (*Psa.* 27:8). Be thou mine, Lord, and I will be thine.' This spiritual answer of the soul comes from the Spirit of God in calling, and it is the first degree of liberty.

Now this answer of the soul, by the power of the Spirit subduing our corruptions, goes together with the obedience of the inward man. For man answers the call not only by the speech of the heart, 'Lord, I do it'; but he indeed does it. And when by the power of the Spirit we come out of the world and out of our corruptions, and walk more freely in the ways of God, we are set at spiritual liberty. Now it is the Spirit who does all this. For if it were not the Spirit that persuaded the soul when the minister speaks, alas! all ministerial persuasions are to no purpose. If the Spirit does not stir up the soul to answer, all speech from men is to no purpose.

But the Spirit does this. First he opens our eyes with spiritual eye-salve to see our natural bondage. He opens our eyes to see, 'I must come out of this condition if I will be saved, or else I will be miserable for ever.' And it is enough for the soul of a miserable man to be convinced of his misery and bondage, of what he is by nature – for let him be convinced of that once, and all the rest of the links of the golden chain of salvation will follow. Let a man be convinced that he is as the Scripture says he is and that it will cost him dearly hereafter; and you shall not need to tell him to leave his worldly course and condition. All this will follow where there is conviction of spirit.

The first work of the Spirit in spiritual liberty, then, is to convince us of sin and misery; and then to work an answer of the soul and an obedience of the whole man.

b) In justification, *the Spirit liberates our conscience from sin.* There is liberty and freedom of conscience from sin and the curse of sin, and all the danger that follows upon sin, by the Spirit.

Objection. But you will say, The liberty of justification is wrought by Christ; we are justified by the obedience of Christ; and the righteousness of Christ is imputed to us.

Answer. It is true that Christ is our righteousness. But what is that to us unless we have something to put it on? Unless we are united to Christ, what good do we have by Christ, if Christ is not ours? If there is not a spiritual marriage, what benefit do we have by him if we do not have him to pay our debt? For his riches to be ours and our debt to be his, there must first be a union.

Now this union is wrought by the Spirit. It is begun in effectual calling. From this union there comes a change: his righteousness is mine, as if I had obeyed and done it myself; and my debts and sins are his. This is by the Spirit, because the union between Christ and me is by the Spirit. For whatever Christ has done, it is nothing to me till there is a union.

And likewise, freedom is by the Spirit, because the Spirit of God works faith in me not only to unite and knit me to Christ, but to persuade me that Christ is mine, that all his is mine, and that my debts are his. The Spirit works this supernatural hand of faith to lay hold upon Christ and then to persuade me. For the Spirit is light, and together with the graces it tells me the graces it works. As reason besides reason, it tells me that I use reason when I do. The Spirit of Christ acts reflexively for, being above reason, it not only lays hold upon Christ, it not only does the work, but it tells me that I do so when I do. So it not only tells me that Christ is mine when I believe, but it assures me that I do believe. It carries a light of its own. I know the light by the light, and reason by reason, and faith by faith. So with this reflexive action, the Spirit brings liberty in justification;

just as it is a means of union by which all that is Christ's becomes mine, and mine becomes Christ's. And likewise it assures me that I do believe, when I do believe without error. For the Spirit is given to me to know the things that I have by Christ, not only the privileges, but the graces.

And unless the Spirit did it, it would never be done, for the soul of man is so full of terrors and fears and jealousies, that unless the Spirit of God witnessed to my spirit that God is reconciled in Christ and that Christ's righteousness is mine, I could never be persuaded of it. For the soul always thinks, God is holiness itself and I am a mass of sin; what reason have I to think that God will be so favourable to such a wretch, to such a lump of sin as I am, were it not for God the Son having satisfied God the Father? God has satisfied God, and the Spirit assures my conscience. So the Spirit, who searches the deep things of God and knows what love is in the heart of God, also searches my spirit. Unless the Spirit should tell me that God the Son has satisfied (and the Father accepts the Son's satifaction), I should never believe it. Therefore God must establish the heart in a gracious liberty of justification, as well as in the fact that God the Son has wrought it.

It is no wonder that men of great ability without grace are full of terrors and despair, for the more cleverness a man has without the Spirit of God, the more he disputes against himself and entangles himself with desperate thoughts. But when the Spirit is brought to speak peace to the soul in Christ, and makes the soul cast itself on him for salvation, then God's Spirit is above the conscience. Though conscience is above all other things, God is above conscience and can still it. And the Spirit tells us that God the Father is reconciled by the death of God the Son. And when God witnesses what God has wrought, then conscience is at peace. We see, then, how the Spirit sets us at liberty in the great matter of justification.

c) In sanctification, *we are liberated from slavery to sin.* In the whole course of a holy life, 'where the Spirit of Christ is, there is liberty' and freedom from the slavery of sin. For the understanding is freed from the bondage of ignorance, the will and affections are freed from the bondage of rebellion; the whole inward and outward man is freed. But this liberty of holiness, inherent liberty, springs from the liberty that we have by justification, by the righteousness of Christ, by which we are perfectly righteous and freed from Satan's claim on us. We are freed from the curse of God and from the law, and enabled in a course of sanctification to go on from grace to grace.

The Spirit of Christ comes after justification. To those to whom God gives forgiveness, he gives his Spirit to sanctify. The same Spirit that assures me of the pardon of my sin sanctifies my nature. The Spirit of sanctification breaks the ruling power of sin. Before then the whole life is nothing but continually sinning and offending God. But now there is a gracious liberty of disposition, a largeness of heart which follows the liberty of condition. When a man is free in condition and law from wrath and the sentence of damnation, then he has a free and voluntary disposition to serve God freely, without fear or constraint.

When a man is under the bondage of the law and under the fear of death with its sting, he does everything with a slavish mind. Where the Spirit of God is, there is the spirit of adoption, the spirit of sons, which is a free spirit. The son does not do his duties to his father out of constraint and fear, but out of nature. The Spirit alters our nature and disposition. It makes us sons, and then we do everything freely. God enlarges the hearts of his children. They can deny themselves for a good work. They are 'zealous of good works'. It is the end of their redemption. We are redeemed to be 'a peculiar people, zealous of good works' (*Titus* 2:14). For then we have a low esteem of all things that hinder us from freeness in God's service, as worldliness, and so on.

What does a Christian do when he sees his gracious liberty in Christ? The love of the world and worldly things – he is ready to part with them all for the service of God. He is so free-hearted that he can part with life itself. Paul says of himself, My life is not dear to me, so I may finish my course with joy (*Acts* 20:24). We see in the martyrs and others how free they were, even of their very blood.

What shall we think, then, of those who, if we get anything of them, it is like getting a spark out of the flint? Duties come from Christians as water out of a spring; they issue naturally, and are not forced, so far as they are spiritual.

I confess that there are remainders of bondage where the Spirit sets at liberty, for while we live in this world there is in us a double principle of nature and grace. Therefore there will be a conflict in every holy duty. When the Spirit would be liberal, the flesh will draw back and say, Oh but I may want! When the Spirit would be most courageous, the flesh will say, But there is danger in it. So there is nothing that we can do without getting it out of the fire. We must resist. But still, here is liberty to do good, because here is a principle that resists the backwardness of the flesh.

In a wicked man there is nothing but flesh, and so there is no resistance. We must understand the nature of this spiritual liberty in sanctification. It is not a liberty freeing us altogether from conflict and deadness and dullness. It is a liberty not freeing us from combat, but enabling us to combat, to fight the battles of the Lord against our own corruptions. Freedom from fighting is the liberty of glory in heaven, when there shall be no enemy within or without.

Therefore Christians must not be discouraged with the stubbornness and unwillingness of the flesh to do good duties. If we have a principle in us to fight against our corruptions, and to get good duties out of ourselves in spite of them, it is an argument for a new nature. God will perfect his own beginnings and subdue the flesh more and more by the power of his Spirit. We see what a sweet excuse our blessed Saviour made for his disciples when they were dead-hearted and drowsy, when they should have comforted him in the garden: 'Oh,' said he, 'the spirit is willing, but the flesh is weak' (*Matt.* 26:41).

Indeed, there is a double hindrance in God's people when they are about holy duties, sometimes from their very mould and nature considered not as corrupted, but the very mould itself. And then consider that as it is made heavier and duller by the flesh and corruptions, there are invincible infirmities and weaknesses in nature. Sometimes after labour and expenditure of energy, deadness creeps in invincibly, and a man cannot overcome those necessities of nature. So the spirit may be willing, and the flesh weak – the flesh without any great corruption. God looks upon our necessities. As we see, Christ made an excuse for his disciples. It was not so much corruption, though that was an ingredient, as nature in itself. Christ saw a great deal of gold in the ore, so we see how he excused them.

Therefore when we are dull, let us strive. Christ is ready to make excuse for us, if our hearts are right. 'The spirit is willing, but the flesh is weak.' I say this for the comfort of the best sort of Christians, who think they are not set at liberty by the Spirit because they find some heaviness and dullness in good duties. As I said, while we live here there is sin in us, but it does not reign. After a man has the Spirit of Christ, the Spirit of Christ maintains a perpetual combat and conflict against sin. It could subdue sin all at once if God saw fit; but God chooses to humble us while we live here and exercise us with spiritual conflicts.

To bring us to heaven God sees it sufficient to set up a combat in us, that we are able by the help of the Spirit to fight God's battles against the flesh. So that the dominion of sin may be broken in us, and excellently, Paul says, 'The law of the spirit of life in Christ Jesus has freed me from the law of sin and death' (*Rom.* 8:2). The law of the Spirit of life, that is, the commanding power of the Spirit of Christ, which commands as a law in the hearts of God's people, frees us from the law, that is, from the commanding power of sin and death. The dominion and tyranny of sin is broken by the Spirit of Christ, so we are set at a gracious liberty. In some respects we are under grace, and sin shall not have dominion over us, as the apostle says.

And by the Spirit of Christ in sanctification we are made kings to rule over our own lusts to some degree. We are not kings to be freed altogether from them, but kings to strive against them. It is a liberty to fight, and in fighting to overcome at last. When the Israelites had a promise that God would give their enemies into their hands, the meaning was not that he would give them without fighting a blow. They would fight, but in fighting they would overcome. So this liberty of sanctification is not a liberty that ends combat with our corruptions, but a gracious liberty to keep them under, till by subduing them little by little, we have a perfect victory. What greater encouragement can a man have to fight against his enemy, than when he is sure of final victory before he fights!

You see then how the Spirit brings liberty into the soul. It brings us out of that cursed kingdom of Satan and sin. It brings us out of the curse of God and the law in justification; and it brings us from the dominion and tyranny of sin by a spirit of sanctification.

But this is not all that is in liberty. For the Spirit frees us not only from sin, but from that which follows it, as fear and terrors of conscience, death and wrath. Now, where the Spirit of God is, it frees from the ill consequences, from the tail that follows sin. Where the Spirit is, it frees us from fear. The same Spirit that tells us in justification that God is appeased also frees us from the fear of damnation and death and judgement, from the terrors of an evil conscience. Being 'sprinkled with the blood of Christ' (*1 Pet.* 1:2), we are freed from fear.

And the Spirit not only frees from the fear of ill things, but frees to do good. Liberty implies two things: a freedom from ill, from a cursed condition, and likewise a liberty to better – a liberty *from* ill, and *to* good. We must understand the breadth of Christ's benefits, because they are complete, not only to free us from ill, but to confer all good to us, as much as our nature is capable of. As much as these souls of ours are capable of, they shall be made free and glorious and happy in heaven. God will leave no part of the soul unfilled, no corner of the soul empty. Little by little he does it, as we shall see in the next verse.

When we are called out of Satan's kingdom we are not only called out of that cursed state, but we are made free to a better kingdom; we are made the members of Christ; we are enfranchised. And so in justification we are not only freed from damnation, from the justice and wrath of God, but we can use the plea of our righteousness by which we have claim to heaven, which is a blessed privilege and prerogative. We are not only free from the curse of the law, but we have other gracious prerogatives and privileges. We are not only freed from the dominion of sin, but we are set at liberty by the Spirit to do what is good. We have a voluntary free spirit to serve God as cheerfully as we served our lusts before.

And as we are freed from the rigour and curse of the law, so we have corresponding prerogatives to good. We are now by the Spirit set at liberty to delight in the law, to make the law our counsellor, to make the Word of God our counsellor. That which terrified and frightened us before is now our direction. A severe schoolmaster to a very young pupil becomes later, as the pupil grows, a wise tutor to guide and direct. So, the law that terrifies and whips us when we are in bondage, till we are in Christ – it scares us to Christ – that law afterward comes to be a tutor, to tell us what we shall do, to counsel us and say this is the best way. And we come to delight in those truths when they are revealed to us inwardly. And the more we know, the more we want to know, because we want to please God better every day.

So besides freedom from what is ill and its consequences, there is a blessed prerogative and privilege. That is what is meant here by liberty. For God's works are complete. We must know when he delivers from ill he advances to good. His works are full works always; he does not do things halfway. We have through Christ and by the Spirit not only freedom from what is ill, but advancement to all that is comforting and graciously good.

Allow me to mention one thing more which, though more subtle, is useful. 'Where the Spirit of God is, there is liberty' of the inward man, liberty of judgement, and liberty of will. Where the Spirit of God is not, there is no liberty, no free will.

That which we call free will is taken either for a natural power or an endowment that God has put upon the soul, and so the will is always free in earth and in hell. The devil's will is free in that way, free to evil. There is natural freedom, for freedom is invested upon the will and God never takes it away.

I do not take freedom to mean acting upon reason to do something, be it good or evil. By freedom I mean ability and strength to do what is good. For any liberty and ability to that which is good is only from the Spirit. The defence of Luther and others who wrote of this freedom is sound and good, that the will of man is slavish altogether without the Spirit of God[1]. 'Where the Spirit is, there is liberty': liberty as it is understood to be power and ability to do good.

A liberty to supernatural objects comes from supernatural principles. Nothing moves above its own sphere; nothing is done above the level of activity that God has put into it. Now a natural man can do nothing except naturally, for nothing can work above itself by its own strength, any more than a beast can work according to the principles of a man. Therefore the soul of man has no liberty at all to that which is spiritually good, without a supernatural principle that raises it above itself and puts it into the rank of supernatural things.

The Spirit of God puts a new life into the soul of a man. When he has done that, that life is preserved against all opposition; and together with preserving that life, it applies that inward life and power to individual works. When we have a new life, we cannot perform particular acts without the inciting power of the Spirit of God. The Spirit stirs us up to every individual thing, when the soul of itself would be inactive. The moving

---

[1]Martin Luther's treatise 'The Bondage of the Will' ('De Servo Arbitrio').

comes from the Spirit of God. As every individual moving in the body comes from the soul, so the Spirit puts a new life, applies that life, and applies the soul to every action. Therefore where the Spirit of God is not, there is no liberty for any supernatural action; but 'where the Spirit of God is, there is liberty'. It follows both negatively and affirmatively. There is a liberty of will for that which is good. So from this it follows again that where the Spirit of God is working efficaciously and effectually, it does not rob the soul of liberty, but perfects that liberty.

Some divines, indeed too many, hold that the Holy Ghost works only by way of persuasion upon the soul, and by way of moving, as it were, from without; but he does not enter into the soul or alter it; he does not work upon the soul as an inward worker, but only as an outward entreater and persuader, suggesting and enticing. But this is too shallow a concept for so deep a business as this, for the Spirit works more deeply than that. It puts a new life into the soul; it takes away the stony heart and gives a heart of flesh (*Ezek.* 11:19). Those phrases of Scripture are too weighty to attach to them such a shallow sense, as only to entreat, as a man would entreat a stone to be warm and to come out of its place. He might entreat long enough. But the Spirit with that speech puts a new life and power, and then acts and stirs that power to all that is good.

Questions of grace and liberty of will

Objection. Oh, say they (which is their main objection), this is detracting from the liberty of the will! This is to overthrow the nature of man!

Answer. Oh, by no means! This is not to diminish the liberty of the will, for the Spirit of God is so wise an agent that he works upon the soul while preserving the principles of a man. It alters the judgement by presenting greater reasons and further light than it saw before. And then, by presenting to the will greater reasons to be good than it ever had to be ill before, it alters the will, so that we will contrary to what we did before. Then when the soul chooses, upon discovery of light and reason, it chooses freely of its own will. The soul does things freely when it does them based upon reason, when judgement says this is good.

Now when the Spirit changes the soul, it presents such strong reasons to come out of its cursed condition and into the blessed estate in Christ, that the will promptly follows what is now understood to be the chief good of all. Here the freedom is preserved, because the will is so stirred by the Holy Ghost, it is as if it stirs itself; and it sees a better good. So grace does not take away liberty. No, it establishes liberty.

We hold that in effectual grace the Spirit of God works upon the soul thoroughly. But still we preserve liberty: we say that the soul works of its own principles, notwithstanding grace, because the Spirit of God acts and leads the soul according to the nature of the soul. The Spirit of God preserves the manner of doing of things, and it is the manner of the reasonable creature to do things freely. The Spirit, though working effectually upon the soul, preserves that mode. And the more effectually it works upon the soul, the more the soul sees reason to do good. So then, the more we give to the Spirit in the question of grace and nature, the more we establish liberty, and do not diminish it.

Even where the Holy Spirit is working mightily, liberty is preserved, as we can observe by the following principles.

The will chooses and inclines according to reason. That must always be the case, or else it is not a human action.

Now when the Spirit of God sets the will at liberty, a man does what he does being fully advised by reason. For though God works upon the will, it is with enlightening of the understanding at the same time. And all grace in the will comes through the understanding, as all heat upon lower things comes with light. So all the work upon the soul is by the heat of the Spirit, but it comes from the light of the understanding. So the freedom of the soul is preserved, because it is with light.

Where freedom is, there is a power to reason on both sides, I may do this or that. That power is always proper to the soul. Now grace does not take away that power to reason on both sides, for when a man is set at liberty to do good from the base slavery of ill, he can reason with himself, 'I might have done this and that if I would be damned.' So judgement is not bound to one thing only, but judgement tells him he might have done otherwise if he had wanted. But he sees he must do this if he does not want to be damned.

Where there is freedom, there is an enlargement to understand more things than one, or else there would be no freedom. Though the soul must choose one thing and not many, yet of itself it has power to choose many things. Some creatures are confined to one thing out of the narrowness of their abilities; some are confined to one thing out of their broadness of ability. These seem contrary, but to clarify I give this instance: the creature that is without reason is always confined to one manner of working, because it lacks understanding to work in any other way. Birds make their nests and bees make their hives always the same way. They have no choice because of their narrow abilities.

Now when the Spirit sets a man at liberty for holy things, he is confined to good; this is true especially in heaven. This is out of breadth of understanding, apprehending many goods and many ills. And that good which, out of a broad understanding, he conceives to be the best good, he is confined to. So though the Spirit of God takes away, as it were, that present liberty that a man cannot do ill – it will not allow him to be so bad as he was – yet it leaves him in a state of good, to do a multitude of good things. And then, though it confines him to a state of happiness so that he cannot will the contrary, still no liberty is taken away, because it is done out of strength of knowledge, not out of narrowness. He judges all things out of broadness, which tells him this is the best of all, and all the soul is carried after it. The glory of heaven does not rob a man of his power.

Why are they confined eternally to that which is good? Is it for lack of understanding that the angels do not choose ill? No! They know what ill is by speculation, but there is a strength of understanding to know what is good. And the understanding, where it has full light, carries the will to choose. Therefore 'where the Spirit of the Lord is, there is liberty'.

Notwithstanding all objections to the contrary, the Spirit does not take away the liberty of the soul; indeed, it strengthens it. It is an idle objection of many who are willing to be deceived. Oh, if grace confines a man, determines him, as the word is, sways him one way perpetually, this confining and swaying one way restricts his liberty, and so on. No; for it comes not from weakness of understanding, but from strength of understanding, and it is perfect liberty to do well. Therefore, on the contrary, it is so far from restricting the liberty of the soul that it cannot do ill or that it can only persevere to do good, that it is the strength of liberty.

Which is greater, the first Adam's liberty, or the liberty in heaven, the second Adam's liberty? Our liberty in grace, or that in glory? The liberty of the first man was that he might not sin if he would; the liberty of Christ was that he could not sin at all. Which do you think was the chief? He that could not, or he that might not sin if he would? Was there not a more gracious and blessed liberty in Christ than in Adam, who might not sin if he would? Is this a worse liberty then, when a man cannot sin? So when the Spirit of God sways the soul and takes away that potentiality and possibility to sin, so that a man cannot sin because he will not, his will is so carried by the strength of judgement, this is the greatest good. 'I will not move out of this circle. If I go out of this I shall be unhappy.' And this is the greatest liberty of all.

What do we pray in the Lord's prayer but for this liberty? 'Thy will be done' (*Matt.* 6:10). That is, take me out of my own will more and more; conform my will to thine in all things. The more I do so, the more liberty I have. The strength of that petition is that we may have perfect liberty in serving God.

The greatest and sweetest liberty is when we have no liberty to sin at all, when we cannot sin. It is greater chastity not to have power to resist, to be impregnable in self-control and sobriety. When there is such a measure of these graces that they cannot be overcome, this is greater strength than when they may be prevailed over.

So men are mistaken to think the greatest liberty is to have power to good or evil. Such power is the imperfection of the creature. Man was at first created free to do either good or evil of himself, that he might fall of himself. This was not strength, but followed from a creature that came out of nothing and was subject to fall to his own principles. But the soul established so that it shall not have freedom to ill is established in good. The understanding is so enlightened and the will so confirmed and strengthened that the soul is without danger of temptation. That is properly glorious liberty, and that is the better endowment of both. We see clearly, then, that grace does not take away liberty, but establishes it.

d) And besides liberty in this world, there is *the liberty of glory*, called 'the liberty of the children of God' (Rom. 8:21): the liberty of our bodies from corruption, *the glorious liberty in heaven, when we shall be perfectly free.* For, alas! in this world we are free to fight, not free from fight. And we are free not from misery but from thraldom to misery. But then we shall be free from the encounter and the encumbrance. 'All tears shall be wiped from our eyes' (*Rev.* 7:17). We shall be free from all physical pain in sickness and infirmity, and free from all the remainders of sin in our souls. That is perfect liberty, perfect redemption, and perfect adoption, both of body and soul.

And by the Spirit we have the beginnings of these in this world, too. For, what is peace of conscience and joy in the Holy Ghost? Is it not the beginnings of heaven, a grape of the heavenly Canaan? Is not the Spirit that we have here a pledge of that inheritance? It is an earnest payment, and an earnest is a piece of the bargain. It is never taken away, but is part of the bargain. So the beginnings of grace and comfort given by the Spirit are the beginnings of that glorious liberty. The earnest assures us of that glorious liberty. For God never goes back on the bargain that he makes with his children. Grace, in some sense, is glory, as we see in the next verse (*2 Cor.* 3:18), because grace is the beginning of glory. It frees the soul from terror and subjection to sin. So the life of glory is begun in grace. We have the life of glory begun by the Spirit, this glorious life.

LIBERTY OF THE GOSPEL

Besides this inward spiritual liberty that we have by the Spirit, there are outward preserving liberties that must be mentioned: a liberty of preaching the gospel, and a liberty of discipline, or government. Government is in the church of God, and should be, because we are men and must have such help. The Spirit bestows these liberties upon the church wherever there is an inward spiritual liberty. Men are brought into the church by the liberty of the gospel and preserved by government. There must be subjection to pastors, and there must be teaching and discipline, or all will be confusion. Now this inward liberty is wrought by the liberty of the gospel.

Question. What is the liberty of the gospel?

Answer. It is a blessed liberty in the church to have true liberty opened, the charter of our liberty.

Question. What is the charter of our liberty?

Answer. The Word of God. When the charter and patent of our liberty is laid open, we come to have a share in those liberties. The liberty of the temple, of the church, of the Word and sacraments, along with order in the church, brings in spiritual liberty and preserves it. It is, as it were, the bonds and sinews of the church. Now where the Spirit of God is with the gospel, there is this liberty of the gospel. The doors of the temple and sanctuary are opened, as, blessed be God, those of this kingdom have been. With spiritual liberty, there is an outward liberty of the tabernacle and house of God: We can all meet to hear the Word of God and receive the sacraments, and we can all meet to call upon God in spirit and in truth. And these outward liberties are blessed liberties, for where God gives them, he intends to bestow and convey spiritual liberty.

[49]

How shall we come to spiritual liberty without unfolding the charter, the Word of God? That is why Christ has established a ministry, apostles, teachers, and pastors to edify the church to the end of the world. So we see, where there is no outward liberty of unfolding the Word, where there is no outward liberty of the ministry, this inward liberty is lacking. For by the preaching of the gospel God sets us at liberty.

When Christ first preached the gospel, it was the year of jubilee. Now in the year of jubilee all servants were set free. This jubilee was a type of the spiritual liberty that the gospel gives. Those who are slaves to sin and Satan, if they will esteem the gracious promises of the gospel, may become the free men of Jesus Christ.

But in those times some preferred to remain servants and not be freed. Their ears were pierced to mark them as perpetual slaves (see *Exod.* 21:2–6). And it is a pity that now, in the glorious jubilee of the gospel, some resolve still to be slaves. When a proclamation of liberty was made that all who wanted could come out of Babylon, many remained there still. So many are in love with Egypt and Babylon and slavery. It is a pity they should be slaves.

But those with more noble spirits, those who desire liberty, should especially desire spiritual liberty. And here you see how to come by it – 'Where the Spirit of the Lord is, there is liberty,' and where the ordinance of God is, that is, the ministry of the Spirit, there is the Spirit. Where these outward liberties are, it is a sign that God intends to set men at spiritual liberty.

Therefore, those who are enemies of dispensing the gospel in the ministry are enemies to spiritual liberty. And it is an argument that when a man is in any way an enemy of the unfolding of the Word of God, he is in bondage to Satan. For it is an argument that he refuses to be called to spiritual liberty, but lives according to the flesh. He will not hear of the liberty of the Spirit, as some men who consider it bondage: 'Let us break their bands, and cast away their cords' (*Psa.* 2:3). Why should we be tied with the Word and with these holy things? It is better that we have no preaching, no order at all, but live every man as he would. Though they do not say this in words, their lives and profane conduct show that they do not esteem outward liberties. They are enemies of that by which spiritual liberty is preserved, and that shows that they are in spiritual bondage, with no share in spiritual liberty.

The gospel is set out by the phrase 'the kingdom of God'. For not only is the kingdom of God set up in our hearts, the kingdom of the Spirit; but where the gospel is preached, there is the kingdom of God. Why? Because with the dispensation of divine truth, Christ comes to rule in the heart. By the outward kingdom comes the spiritual kingdom. They come under one name.

Those who would have the spiritual kingdom of God to rule in their hearts by grace and peace till they reign for ever in heaven must come by this door – by the ministry, by the outward ordinance. The ordinance brings them to grace, and grace to glory. It is a good and sweet sign of a man spiritually set at liberty, brought out of the kingdom of Satan and freed from the guilt and dominion of sin, when he can meekly and cheerfully submit to the ordinance of God with a desire to have spiritual duties unfolded and the riches of Christ laid open. When he hears these things with a relish and a love, using the charter of his soul so well, it is a sign God loves his soul and that he has a share in spiritual liberty. 'Where the Spirit of the Lord is, there is liberty.'

USES

Use 1. If all the blessed liberties in this world and in that to come are by the Spirit, let us labour to have the Spirit of Christ, or else we have no liberty at all.

Let us strive more and more every day to have this spiritual liberty in our consciences, to be assured by the Spirit that our sins are forgiven, and to feel a power to subdue the sin that has tyrannized us before. Let us labour more and more every day to find this spiritual liberty, and daily prize more the ordinances of God, sanctified to set us at liberty. Attend upon spiritual means, which God has sanctified and by which he will convey the Spirit. There were times when an angel came to stir the waters of the pool (*John* 5:4). So the Spirit of God stirs the waters of the Word and ordinances, and makes them effectual. If we attend upon the ordinances of God and the communion of saints, the Spirit of God will slide into our souls in the use of holy means. There is no man who does not experience this. He finds himself raised above himself in the use of holy means.

The more we know the gospel, the more we have of the Spirit; and the more Spirit we have, the more liberty we enjoy. If we prize and value outward liberty, as indeed we do naturally, how we should prize the charter of our spiritual liberty, the Word of God, and the promises of salvation. It is by these we come to know all our liberty and where all the promises are opened to us: the promise of forgiveness of sins, of necessary grace, of comfort in all conditions whatever. Therefore let us every day labour to grow more and more both in the knowledge and in the taste and feeling of this spiritual liberty.

Use 2. Oh, what a blessed condition it is to have this spiritual liberty!

Do see its blessed use and comfort in all conditions.

For if a man has the Spirit of God to set him at liberty, he has the Spirit of God to free him from temptation. Or if temptation catches hold of him so that he sins, he has the Spirit of God to fly to, the blood of Christ, to show that if he confesses his sins and lays hold on Christ, he has pardon for sin. And the blood of Christ 'speaks better things than the blood of Abel'. It speaks mercy and peace. If by faith he sprinkles it upon his soul, if he knows the liberty of justification and makes use of it, what a blessed liberty this is when we have sinned!

If ever God restrains us in the outward man to humble us, what a blessed thing it is that the spirit is at liberty! A man may have a free conscience and mind in a restrained condition; and a man may be restrained in a free state. In the guilt of sin, bound over to the wrath of God, and bound over to another evil day, a man in the greatest subjection may have liberty. What a blessed condition this is!

Also in sickness, consider the glorious liberty of the sons of God, a redemption of body as well as of soul, that these base bodies of ours shall be like Christ's glorious body. The resurrection will make amends for all these bodily sicknesses and ills – what a comfort it is to think of the resurrection to glory!

And when death comes, we know that by the blood of Christ there is a liberty to enter into heaven, that Christ by his blood has opened a passage to heaven.

And so in all necessities we have a liberty to the throne of grace; we are free in regard to heaven; free in the company of saints in earth and in heaven too; free to have communion with God. We have a freedom in all the promises. What a sweet thing this is, in all wants and necessities, to use a spiritual liberty, to have the ear of God as a favourite in heaven – not only to be free from the wrath of God, but to have his favour, to have his care in all our necessities. What a blessed liberty this is, that a man may go with boldness to the throne of grace by the Spirit of Christ!

Oh, it is invaluable. There is not the least part of this spiritual liberty that is not worth a thousand worlds. How we should value it and bless God for giving Christ to work this blessed liberty, and for giving his Spirit to apply it to us more and more and to set us more and more at spiritual liberty. For the Father, the Son, and the Holy Ghost all join in this spiritual liberty. The Father gives the Son, and he gives the Spirit – and all to set us free. It is a comforting and blessed condition.

Use 3. But how shall we know whether or not we are set at liberty?
Everyone will claim to have liberty from the law and from the curse of God and his wrath in justification. And though that is the foundation of all, I will not speak of that, but of that which always accompanies it: a liberty of holiness, a liberty to serve God, a liberty from bondage to lusts and to Satan.

a) Wherever the Spirit of God is, there is a *liberty of holiness, to free us from the dominion of any one sin*. We are freed 'to serve him in holiness all the days of our lives' (*Luke* 1:74–75). Where the Spirit is, therefore, it will free a man from enslavement to sin, even to any one sin. The Spirit reveals to the soul the odiousness of the bondage. For a man to be a slave to Satan, who is his enemy, a cruel enemy, what an odious thing this is! Now whoever is captive to any lust is in captivity to Satan by that lust. Therefore where this liberty is, there cannot be slavery to any one lust.

Satan does not care how many sins one forsakes if he still lives in any one sin, for by one sin he has him and can pull him in. Children when they have a bird can let it fly, but it is on a string to be pulled back again. So Satan has men on a string, if they live in any one sin. The Spirit of Christ is not there, but Satan's spirit, and he can pull them in when he wants. The beast that runs away with a cord about him is caught by the cord again. So when we forsake many sins yet still carry his cords about us, he can pull us in when he wants. Such prisoners are at liberty more than others, but they are slaves to Satan by that. And where Satan keeps possession and rules there by one sin, there is no liberty. For the spirit of sanctification is an antedote to the corruption of nature, and it opposes it in all the powers of the soul. It allows no corruption to have control.

b) Where this liberty from the Spirit is, there is not only a freedom from all gross sins, but a *blessed freedom to do all duties with a full heart*. God's people are a willing people. Those under grace are anointed by the Spirit (*Psa.* 89:20), and that spiritual anointing makes them active. Now he that is truly anointed by the Spirit is in some degree quick and active in what is good.

One result of anointing is to give agility and strength. So the Spirit of God is a spirit of cheerfulness and strength. Finding cheerfulness and strength to perform holy services, to hear the Word, to pray to God, and to perform holy duties – this comes from the Spirit of God. The Spirit sets people at this liberty, because otherwise spiritual duties are as opposite to flesh and blood as fire is to water.

When we are drawn to duties out of wrong motives or fear or custom, and not from a new nature, this is not from the Spirit, and their performance is not from the true liberty of the Spirit. For under the liberty of the

Spirit, actions come off naturally, not forced by fear or hope or any extra motives. A child does not need other motives to please his father. When he knows he is the child of a loving father, it is natural. So there is a new nature in those who have the Spirit of God to stir them up to duty, though God's motives of sweet encouragements and rewards may help. But the principal is to do things naturally, not out of fear or to appease other people.

Artificial things move from a principle outside themselves. Clocks and such things have weights that move all the wheels they go by. So it is with an artificial Christian who sets himself to a course of religion. He moves by weights outside himself, and does not have an inward principle of the Spirit to make things natural to him, to excite him and make him do things naturally and sweetly. 'Where the Spirit of God is, there is freedom' – that is, a kind of natural freedom, not forced, not moved by any alien motive.

c) With the freedom of spirit, there is *courage and strength of faith against opposition*. When the Spirit reveals with conviction the excellence of the state we are in, and the vileness of the state we are moved to by opposition – what is all opposition to a spiritual man? It gives him courage and strength to resist. The more opposition, the more courage he has. When the early Christians had the Spirit of God (*Acts* 4:23ff), they resisted opposition, and the more they were opposed, the more they grew. They were cast in prison, and rejoiced. And the more they were imprisoned, the more courageous they were still.

There is no setting against this wind or quenching of this fire by any human power, where it is true; for the Spirit of God, where it truly sets a man at liberty, gathers strength by opposition. See how the Spirit triumphed in the martyrs over fire, and imprisonment, and all opposition. The Spirit in them set them at liberty from such base fears that it prevailed in them over all. The Spirit of God is a victorious Spirit, freeing the soul from base fears of any creature. 'If God be for us, who can be against us?' (*Rom.* 8:31).

It is said of Stephen that they could not withstand the Spirit by which he spoke (*Acts* 6:10). And Christ promises a Spirit that no enemies shall be able to withstand. So God's children, in the time of opposition, when they understand themselves and what they stand for, are given by God a Spirit against which no enemies can stand. The Spirit of Christ in Stephen put such a glory upon him that he looked as if he were an angel (*Acts* 6:15). The Spirit of liberty gives boldness, strength and courage against opposition. Those, therefore, who are daunted by every small thing when standing in a good cause do not have the Spirit of Christ; for where that is, it frees men from these fears, especially if the cause is God's.

d) The Spirit of liberty gives *boldness with God himself*, who otherwise is a 'consuming fire' (*Heb.* 12:29). The Spirit of Christ goes through the mediation of Christ to God. Christ, by his Spirit, leads us to God. Those who do not have the Spirit of God cannot go to God with a spirit of boldness. Therefore, it is in the time of temptation or great affliction, especially when there is opposition, that a man may best judge what he truly is. When a man is in temptation from within or without, or opposition from the world, and can go boldly to God and pour out his soul to God freely as to a father, this comes from the Spirit of liberty. One without the Spirit of Christ, even with great abilities or strength, can never do this. In the time of extremity, he sinks. But a child of God in extremity has a spirit to go in a familiar manner to God, and to cry, Abba, Father.

Saul was a mighty man. But when he was in anguish, he could not go to God. Cain could not go to God. Judas, a man of great knowledge, could not go to God. His heart was wicked; he did not have the Spirit of Christ, but the spirit of the devil. And the spirit of bondage bound him over for his treason to hell and destruction, because he did not have the Spirit to go to God, but accounted him his enemy; he had betrayed Christ. If he had said as much to God as he did to the scribes and Pharisees, he might have had mercy in the force of the event. I am speaking not of the decree of God, but of the nature of the act itself: if he had said so much to Christ and to God, he might have found mercy.

So let a man be ever so great a sinner – if he can go to God, spread his soul, and lay open his sins with any remorse; if he can come in confession and petition and beg mercy of God in Christ to shine as a Father upon his soul – this Spirit of liberty to go to God argues that the Spirit of Christ is there. In Romans 8:26, which speaks of comfort in afflictions, one comfort among the rest is that the children of God have the Spirit of God, to stir up sighs and groans. Now, where the Spirit of God stirs up sighs and groans, God understands the meaning of his own Spirit. There is the spirit of liberty and there is the spirit of sons, for a spirit of liberty is the spirit of a son. A man may know that he is a son of God and a member of Christ. And he may know that he has the spirit of liberty in him, if in affliction and trouble he can sigh and groan to God in the name and mediation of Christ.

That familiar boldness by which we cry, Abba, Father, comes from being sons; only they can cry so. This comes from the Spirit. If we are sons, then we have the Spirit by which we cry, Abba, Father. So, if we can go to God with a sweet familiarity – Father, have mercy upon me, forgive me; look in the depths of pity upon me – this sweet boldness and familiarity comes from the Spirit of liberty and shows that we are sons, and not illegitimate.

Your strong, rebellious, sturdy-hearted persons, who think to work out of their misery by the strength of abilities and friends, die in despair. Their sorrows are too much for them. But when a broken soul goes to God in Christ with boldness, this opening of the soul to God is a sign of liberty, of the liberty of sons. For this liberty is the liberty of sons, of a spouse, of kings, of members of Christ; it is the sweetest liberty that can be imagined. It is the liberty that those sweet relations breed, that of a wife to the husband, of loving subjects to their prince, and of children to their father. Here is a sweet liberty; and where the Spirit of God is, there is all this sweet liberty.

A man who is on the way to heaven may be in any of three states:

i) The state of nature, when he cares about neither heaven nor hell, so he may have sensual nature pleased and go on without fear or wisdom; without grace, indeed, without the principles of nature, so he may satisfy himself in a course of sin. That is the worst state, the state of nature.

ii) But God, if he belongs to him, will not allow him to be in this brutish condition long; he brings him under the law. That is, he sets a man's own corrupt nature before him and shows him the course of his life. Then he is afraid of God: 'Depart from me; I am a sinner .' As Adam, when he had sinned, ran from God, who was sweet to him before; so a brute man, when his conscience is awakened to sin, when he considers that there is but a step between him and hell, and considers what a God he has to deal with and that after death there is eternal damnation – when the Spirit of God has convinced him of this, then he is in a state of fear. And in this state, he is unfit to have liberty to run to God. He uses all his power to move away from God all he can, and hates God, and wishes there were no God, and trembles at the very thought of God and of death.

iii) Oh, but if a man belongs to God, God will not leave him in this condition either (though this is better than the first; it is better that a man be out of his wits almost, than to be senseless as a block). But there is another condition, and that is the condition of liberty, when God by his Spirit reveals to him in Christ forgiveness of sins, the gracious face of God ready to receive him: 'Come unto me, all ye that are weary and heavy laden' (*Matt.* 11:28), says Christ; and 'where sin has abounded, grace more abounds' (*Rom.* 5:20). When a man hears this still, sweet voice of the gospel, he begins to take comfort to himself, and then he goes to God freely.

Now all those in this state of freedom, even at their worst, have boldness to go to God. David in his extremity runs to God. David trusted in the Lord his God. What does Saul do at his wits' end? He runs to his sword's point (*1 Sam.* 31:4). Take a man under nature, or under the law, in extremity: the greater wit he has, the more he entangles himself. His wit serves to entangle him, to weave a web of his own despair. But take a gracious man who is acquainted with God in Christ: in such a man at the lowest there is a liberty to go to God, for he has the Spirit of Christ in him. What did the Spirit in Christ himself direct him to do at the lowest? 'My God, my God' (*Mark* 15:34). In the deepest desertion, he could yet say, 'My God'. There was a liberty to go to God. So take a Christian that has the same Spirit in him, as indeed he has: he can say, 'My God' still. He owns God and knows him in all extremity.

Many at times like these are found to have no Spirit of God in them. In trouble, where do they go? To their purse, to their friends, to anything. They labour to overcome their troubles one way or another, by medications and the like, but never go with boldness and comfort and familiarity to God. They have no familiarity with God; therefore they do not have a Spirit of liberty.

e) Again, where this Spirit of liberty is, there is a *freedom from common prevailing notions*, from the errors and the slavish courses of the times. There are two sorts of wicked persons in the world: one sort count it their heaven and happiness to domineer over others, to bring them into subjection, and to rule over their consciences if they can, so they will sell all to please them. The other sort will sell their liberty, their reason and everything for even a poor thing, so they may get anything that they value in the world. They are made beasts, as if they had no reasonable understanding souls, much less grace. Between those two, some domineering and others servile, a few that live upon terms of Christianity are of sound judgement.

Now where the Spirit of God is, there is liberty, that is, a freedom not to enslave our judgements, much less conscience, to any man. The judgement of man enlightened by reason is above any creature. Reason is a beam of God, and all the persons in the world ought not to have power over a man to make him say what he knows to be untrue. That is to speak against God, even if only in civil matters or anything else. Judgement is the spark of God. Nature is but God's candle, a light of the same light which provides grace, but it is inferior.

If a man speaks against his conscience – enslaves his conscience – to please men, where is liberty? No man that has the spirit of a man will say as another man says, will judge as another man judges, and will do all as another man does, without seeing some reason for doing so himself. That is true of a man as a man, unless he wants to dehumanize himself.

It is much more true of a Christian man. He will not enslave his conscience out of fear, or sell heaven and happiness and his comfort for this and that. And those who do, though they talk of liberty, are slaves. Though they may domineer in the world, the curse of Ham is upon them; they are slaves of slaves (*Gen.* 9:25).

Therefore, where the Spirit of Christ is, there is a liberty of independence. A man is not dependent upon any other man, beyond what agrees with the rules of religion. He is dependent only upon God and upon divine principles and grounds. The apostle says, 'The spiritual man judgeth all things, but is judged of none' (*1 Cor.* 2:15). So far as a man is 'led by the Spirit' (*Rom.* 8:14), he discerns things in the light of the Spirit. He judges all things to be as they are, in the light of the Spirit, and is judged of none.

The apostle does not mean that no one will usurp judgement of him, for that they will do – the emptiest men are most rash and critical – but he is judged of none rightly. But the spiritual man indeed passes a right verdict upon persons and things, as far as he is spiritual. And that is the reason that carnal men especially hate spiritual men above all things. They hate men who have a natural conscience, who judge according to the light of reason, for that is above any creature. A man with a natural conscience will not say that white is black, that good is evil, to please anyone in the world. And this is very distasteful. Where men idolize themselves, they do not love such men, but they love those who are slaves to them.

But much more, when a man is spiritual, he judges all things and censures them; for he is above all, and sees all beneath him. The greatest men in the world are holy men. They are above all others, and without usurpation they pass censure upon the state of other men, even the greatest of them. However the image of God is upon these others with regard to their authority and the like, in their dispositions they are base, and slaves to their corruptions and to Satan. They are not out of the low rank of nature.

Now a man who is a child of God is taken into a better condition and has spiritual liberty in him. 'He judges all things and is judged of none.' They may call him this and that, but it is malice, a trace of the sin against the Holy Ghost. But their hearts tell them he is otherwise. He shall judge them before long, for the saints shall judge the world (*1 Cor.* 6:3, *Matt.* 19:28). Therefore Christians should know, and take notice of, their excellency. 'Where the Spirit of God is, there is liberty' to judge all things as far as they come within their reach and calling, and to judge them rightly. We should know how to maintain the credit of a Christian, the liberty independent of all but God, and independent of other things as far as it agrees with conscience and religion.

The apostle does not say there is licence to shake off all regulation, for by too much licence all liberty is lost; but 'where the *Spirit of God is, there* is liberty'. A true Christian is the greatest servant and the greatest freeman in the world. He has a spirit that will yield to none. In things spiritual he reserves a liberty for his judgement, yet for outward conformity of life he is a servant to all, to do them good. Love makes him a servant. Christ was the greatest servant that ever was. He was both the servant of God and our servant. And there is none so free. The greater portion of the Spirit, the more inward and spiritual freedom. And the more freedom, the more disposition to serve one another in love, to do all things that a man should do outwardly, all things that are lawful.

We must take heed that we do not mistake this spiritual liberty. It conforms to all good laws and all good orders, and carnal men make a great mistake in thinking it is liberty to do as they choose. It is true, if a man has a strong and a holy understanding. But it is the greatest bondage in the world to have most freedom in ill. As I said before, those who are most free in ill are the greatest slaves of all. Their corruptions will not allow them to hear good things, to be where good things are spoken, to keep company with those who are good, because their corruptions have them in so narrow a custody. The corruptions of some men are so malignant and binding that they will not allow them to be in any circumstance in which their corruptions may be restrained at all, and they hate the very thought of persons and all laws that might restrain them. This is the greatest slavery in the world, for a man to have no acquaintance with that which is contrary to his corrupt disposition.

Well, 'new lords, new laws': the moment a man is in Christ and has Christ's Spirit, he has another law in his soul to rule him contrary to that which there was before. Before he was ruled by the law of his lusts, which carried him where it would. But now in Christ he has a new Lord and a new law, and that rules him according to the government of the Spirit. 'The law of the Spirit of life in Christ has freed me from the law of sin and death' (*Rom.* 8:2).

Use 4. Again, seeing this sweet and glorious liberty, let us take heed by all means that we do not grieve the Spirit.

When we find the Holy Ghost in the use of any good means to touch upon our souls, O give him entrance and way to come into his own chamber, as it were, to provide a room for himself when he knocks. We who live in the church, the heart of each one of us, without exception, tells us that we have often resisted the Holy Ghost. We might have been saved if we had not been rebellious and opposing. Do not grieve the Spirit by any means.

The Spirit may be grieved in any of several ways. As the Spirit is a Spirit of holiness, he is grieved with unclean intentions, words, and actions. He is called the *Holy* Spirit, and as he breathes into us holy promptings, he breathes out of us good, holy and savoury words, stirring us up to holy actions. Now when we give liberty to our mouths to speak in a coarse and filthy way, is this not grieving the Spirit, if we have the Spirit at all? If we do not care about grieving ourselves, do we not grieve everyone about us? Take heed, then, of all filthy, unholy words, thoughts, or behaviour. They grieve the Spirit.

As the Spirit is a Spirit of love, let us take heed against bitterness and malice. We grieve the Spirit of God by cherishing bitterness and malice against one another. They drive away the sweet spirit of love. Therefore be conscious of grieving the Spirit. He who is the Spirit of love will not rest in a malicious heart.

Those who are filled with vain, high, proud conceit grieve and keep out the good Spirit of God. The Spirit of Christ is joined with a spirit of humility. 'God gives grace to the humble' (*James* 4:6). The Spirit empties the soul of its windy vanity in order to fill it with itself. We should empty our souls that the Spirit of God may have a large dwelling there, or else we grieve the Spirit.

Any sin against conscience grieves the Spirit of God

and hinders spiritual liberty, because 'where the Spirit of God is, there is liberty'. If we would preserve liberty, we must preserve the Spirit. If we sin against conscience, we hinder liberty in every way. We hinder our liberty to do good duties. When a man sins against conscience, he is dead to good actions. His conscience says, 'How can you go about it, when you have done this or that bad thing?' He is shackled in his performances; he cannot go so naturally to prayer or to hear sermons.

Conscience obstructs him, first, by shackling him in prayer. He does not have liberty to go to the throne of grace. How can he dare look to heaven, when he has grieved the Spirit of God and broken the peace of his conscience? What communion does he have with God? So it hinders peace with God. A man cannot look Christ in the face. As when a man is ashamed to look on another whom he has wronged, so the soul that has run into sins against conscience is ashamed to look on Christ and to go to God again. Any sin against conscience grieves the Spirit and hinders all sweet liberty that was there before.

It also hinders boldness with men. For what makes a man courageous in his dealings with men? A clear conscience. Even the bravest man in the world, if he maintains any sin against conscience, is made a slave. For when it comes to giving in to that lust once, then you shall see he will even betray all his former boldness and strength. If a man is covetous and ambitious, he may be courageous and bold for a time, but it will take away all liberty that he has, to cherish any sin.

In a word, *to preserve this liberty, let us go to Christ,* from whom we have this liberty, and complain to him. When we find any corruption stirring, go to the Lord in the words of St Augustine and say, 'Now, Lord, free me from my necessities.' 'I cannot serve thee as I should do, nor as I would do. I am enslaved to sin, but I want to do better. I cannot do as well as I would; free me from my necessities.' Let us complain of our corruptions to God. As the woman in the law, who complained if she was assaulted and so saved her life (*Deut.* 22:25-27), let us complain to Christ if we find violence offered to us by our corruptions. 'I cannot by my own strength set myself at liberty from this corruption. Lord, give me thy Spirit to do it. Set me more and more at liberty from my former bondage and from this that has enslaved me.' So complain to Christ, and desire him to do his office. 'Lord, thy office is "to destroy the works of the devil"' (*1 John* 3:8).

And go to the Spirit. It is the office of the Holy Ghost to free us, to be a Spirit of liberty. Now desire Christ and the Holy Ghost to do their office of setting us at spiritual liberty. And this we must do also by the use of means and by avoiding certain situations, and then it will be efficacious to preserve the spiritual liberty that will tell our consciences that we are not hypocrites, and that will end in a glorious liberty in the life to come.

And let this be a comfort to all poor struggling and striving Christians who are not yet set at perfect liberty from their lusts and corruptions: that it is the office of the Spirit of Christ as the king of the church, by his Spirit, to purge the church perfectly, to make it a glorious spouse. And at last he will fulfil his own office.

And besides this liberty of grace joined with conflict in this world, there is another liberty of glory, when we shall be freed from all oppositions without and from all conflict and corruption within. It is called 'the liberty of the sons of God' (*Rom.* 8:21). Those who are not looking more and more for the gracious liberty to be free from passions and corruptions here must not look for the glorious liberty in heaven. But those who live a conflicting life, and pray to Christ more and more for the Spirit of liberty to set up a liberty in them, these may look for the liberty of the Son of God which will be before long, when we shall be out of reach and free from corruption, when the Spirit of God shall be all in all. Now our lusts will not allow the Spirit to be all in all, but in heaven he shall. There shall be nothing to rise against him.

4: *The Gospel Is beyond the Law*

'But we all, as in a glass, with open face behold the glory of the Lord, and are changed into the same image, from glory to glory, as by the Spirit of the Lord.'

As the sun rises by degrees till it comes to shine in glory, so it was with the Sun of righteousness. He revealed himself in the church little by little. The latter times now are more glorious than the former. And because comparisons give lustre, the blessed apostle compares the administration of the covenant of grace under the gospel with that of the same covenant in the time of the law, and by comparison he shows the administration under the gospel to be more excellent. Besides other differences in this chapter, the apostle emphasises these especially.

'We all with open face . . .' Only Moses beheld the glory of the Lord in the mount, but 'we all' – not all men, but all sound Christians who have their eyes opened, all sorts of believers – behold this glory. In spiritual things there is no basis for envy, for everyone may partake of everything. In the things of this life there is envy, because the more one has, the less another has. But for more to partake of spiritual things is a matter of glory and excellency. The Jews rejoiced that the Gentiles should be called, and we now rejoice in hope, and should rejoice marvellously if we could see it effected, that the Jews should be taken in again. The more there are, the better it is. 'We all'.

'*We behold with open face,*' that is, with freedom and boldness, which was not true in the time of the law. They were afraid to look upon Moses when he came down from the mount, his countenance was so majestic and terrifying. But 'we all with open face'– freely, boldly, and joyfully – look upon the glory of God in the gospel. The light of the gospel is attracting and comforting; the light of the law was dazzling and terrifying.

And we behold '*as in a glass*'. They beheld God as in a glass, or mirror, but it was not so clear a glass. They beheld him, as it were, in the water; we behold him in crystal. We see God in the glass of the Word and sacraments, but they saw him in a world of ceremonies. To them Christ was swaddled and wrapped up in a great many types.

'*We are changed from glory to glory.*' The gospel is beyond the law. The law did not have power to convert, to change people into its own likeness. But now the gospel, which is the ministry of the Spirit, has power to transform and change them into the likeness of Christ, whom it preaches. It is a gradual change, not all at once, but from glory to glory, from one degree of grace to another; for grace is here called glory. We are changed from the state of grace till we come to heaven, the state of glory.

And the cause of all is '*the Spirit of the Lord*'. The Spirit runs through all. It is 'by the Spirit of the Lord' that we behold. It is the Spirit of the Lord that takes away the veil. It is by the Spirit that we are changed from glory to glory.

We see how the administration of the covenant of grace now surpasses its administration then. It gives liberty and freedom from the bondage of ceremonies and of the law. We have more freedom and liberty. We see Christ more clearly. The Spirit works more strongly now, working to change. We are changed from the heart, inwardly and thoroughly. The gospel extends grace to all, Gentiles as well as Jews.

So let us seriously and fruitfully consider what excellent times the Lord has set us in, and respond thankfully and obediently. God has reserved us to these glorious times, better than our forefathers ever saw.

There are three main parts of the text:

- Our communion and fellowship with God in Christ. 'We all now in a glass behold the glory of the Lord';
- Our conformity to him. By beholding we are changed into the same image;
- The cause of both. 'Beholding the glory of the Lord' and 'being changed from glory to glory' are by the Spirit of God.

This text refers many times to glory. All is glorious in it. There is the glorious mercy of God in Christ, who is the Lord of glory; the gospel in which we see the grace of God and of Christ, 'The glorious gospel' (*1 Tim.* 1:11); the change by which we are changed, a glorious change 'from glory to glory', and by a glorious power, by 'the Spirit of the Lord'; all here is glorious. Therefore blessed be God, and blessed be Christ, and blessed be the Spirit, and blessed be the gospel, and we are blessed that live in these blessed and glorious times!

The happiness of man consists in communion with God and conformity to him. The means to attain both are laid down in this verse, and I shall take them in order.

5: *Our Communion and Fellowship with God in Christ*

'But we all, as in a glass, with open face behold the glory of the Lord.'

Two things must be considered here. The first is that of God's disclosing himself by his Spirit. This is what is meant by 'the glory of the Lord . . . in a glass'. The second is our apprehension of him: 'beholding' that glory. In the glass of the gospel we see Christ, and in Christ the glory of God shining, especially his mercy.

The grace and free mercy of God are his glory. Now in our fallen state, the glory of God is especially his mercy shining in Jesus Christ.

What is glory? It implies these things:

Excellence. Nothing is glorious but that which is excellent.

Evidence and manifestation. Nothing is glorious, even though excellent, if it does not appear to be so. Therefore light is said to be glorious, because the rays of it appear and shine into the eyes of all. And therefore, to describe glory, we use terms pertaining to light, such as 'illustrious' and 'bright', because where glory is there must be manifestation. Thus light is a creation of God that manifests both itself and other things.

Victory. In glory there is such a degree of excellence that it is victorious and convincing, conquering what opposes it. Light causes darkness to vanish immediately. When the sun, that glorious creation, appears, where are the stars? And where are inferior men in the presence of a glorious prince? They are hidden. The inferior things are overshadowed by glory.

Approval by others. Usually glory has the approval of others, or else it has not achieved its right end. Why does God create such glory in nature as light, but so that men may behold it? And why are kings and great men glorious at certain times, but that men may see? If there were no beholders, there would be no glory.

'THE GLORY OF THE LORD'

Now to apply this to the point in hand: 'The glory of the Lord'– that is, his attributes, especially grace, mercy, and love in Christ – this is his excellence. And there is evidence and manifestation of it. It appears to us in Christ. In him 'the grace of God has appeared' (*Titus* 2:11). Christ is called grace. He is the grace of God clothed with man's nature. When Christ appeared, the grace and mercy and love of God appeared. Then again, it is victorious, shining to victory over all that opposes it. For, alas, what would become of us if there were not grace above sin, and mercy above misery, and power in Christ Jesus above all the power in Satan and death? And those who belong to God have a testimony of all this. For they have their eyes opened to behold this glory, and by beholding are transformed from glory to glory, as we shall see.

So whatever may be said of glory may be said of 'the glory of the Lord', from which all other glory indeed is derived. And by the glory of the Lord, then, is meant especially the glory of his mercy and love in Jesus Christ.

The various attributes of God shine upon different occasions. There are, as it were, several theatres in which their glory is revealed. In creation there was, most of all, power; in governing the world, wise providence; in hell, justice in punishing sinners. But now to man in a lapsed state, what attribute shines most and is most glorious? Oh, it is mercy and free grace. If grace and mercy were hidden, our state being as it has been since the fall, what would all other attributes be but a cause for terror? To think of the wisdom and power and justice of God would add to the terror. He is the wiser and more powerful and can take revenge on us. But grace is the glorious attribute by which God sets himself to triumph over the greatest evil that can be, over sin. That which is worse than the devil himself could not prevail over his grace. There is more height and depth and breadth, there are greater dimensions in love and mercy in Christ, than there are in our sins and miseries. And all this is gloriously revealed in the gospel.

Do you wonder why the grace of God has found such enemies as it always has, especially in religions in which works are mingled with grace? It is because the contrary heart of man, being in a frame of enmity to God, sets itself most against that which God will be glorified in. Therefore we should labour to vindicate nothing so much as grace. A dangerous encroaching sect has risen up, enemies to the grace of God, who cover their plot cleverly and closely; but they set nature against grace. Let us vindicate that upon all occasions. For we live by grace, and we must die by grace and stand at the day of judgement by grace – not in our own righteousness, but in the righteousness of Christ, being found in him.

Because it is a point that may serve us all, let us consider how God will honour himself gloriously in this sweet attribute and how the glory of God shines in Christ more than in other ways. We will do so by way of comparison.

[74]

The glory of God was in Adam. Adam had the image of God upon him and had communion and fellowship with God. But there is greater glory now shining in the gospel, in Jesus Christ, to poor sinners. For when man stood in innocence, God did good to a good man, and God was amiable and friendly to a friend. Adam was the friend of God then. Now to do good to one who is good and to maintain sweet communion with a friend is good indeed, and it was a great glory of God's mercy that he would raise such a creature as man to that height.

But now in Jesus Christ there is a further glory of mercy, for God does good to evil men, and the goodness of God is victorious and triumphant over the greatest misery and the greatest ill of man. Now in the gospel God does good to his greatest enemies (*Rom.* 5:10). God set forth and gloriously commended his love, that 'when we were enemies, he gave his Son for us'. Therefore greater glory of mercy and love shines forth to fallen man in Christ than to Adam in innocence.

The glory of God shines in the heavens. 'The heavens declare the glory of God, and the firmament shows his handiwork'(*Psa.* 19:1). Every creature has a beam of God's glory in it. The whole world is a theatre of the glory of God. But what is the glory of creation, of the preservation and governing of the world, compared to the glory of his mercy and compassion that shines in Christ? The glory of the creature is nothing to this, for all the creatures were made of nothing. But the glory of mercy is such in Christ that God became a creature himself.

But to go higher, *consider the angels themselves.* It is not *philangelia*, the love of angels, but *philanthropia*, the love of humans, that outshines all. God is not called the lover of angels. He took upon himself not the nature of angels, but the nature of man; and man is the spouse of Christ, the member of Christ. Angels are not so. They are but ministering spirits for the good of those who shall be saved. Christ, when he rose again, was advanced above all principalities and powers (*Eph.* 1:21), and so above angelic nature.

Now Christ and the church are all one. They make but one mystical body. The church is the queen, and Christ is the king. Therefore Christ mystical, the church, is above all angelic nature whatever. The angels are not the queen and spouse of Christ. But God has dignified and advanced our nature in Jesus Christ. So the glory of God's goodness is more to man, to sinful man, after he believes and is made one with Christ, than to any creature whatever. Here is a glory with excellency.

Nothing is more terrifying than to consider that without regard to Christ, God is a 'consuming fire' (*Heb.* 12:29). But nothing is sweeter than to consider his glorious mercy in Jesus Christ. For in Jesus Christ God has taken the relation of a Father, 'the Father of mercies, and God of all comfort' (*2 Cor.* 1:3). The nature of God is lovely in Christ, and our nature in Christ is lovely to him. And this made the angels, when Christ was born, to sing from heaven, 'Glory to God on high' (*Luke* 2:14). They themselves do not enjoy the grace by Christ, but enjoyed increase of comfort and glory when Christ was born. What glory? Why, the glory of his mercy, of his love, of his grace to sinful men. Indeed, there is a glory of wisdom to reconcile justice and mercy, and a glory of truth to fulfil the promise.

But what set to work all his attributes for our salvation were mercy and grace. That is the glory of God especially meant here. For as we say with regard to morality, that is the greatest virtue that other virtues serve; so in divinity, that attribute which others serve is the greatest of all. In our salvation, wisdom and indeed justice itself serve mercy. For God by his wisdom devised a way to satisy justice. He sent his Son to take our nature, and in that nature to give satisfaction to justice, that there might be a harmony among the attributes.

USES

Does God manifest his glory of grace and mercy in the gospel? Does he show such glorious mercy in Christ? Then:

Use 1. Let us, I beseech you, justify God and this course that he has taken to glorify his mercy in Jesus Christ, by embracing Christ.
It is said that the proud Pharisees 'despised the counsel of God' (*Luke* 7:30). God has poured out abundant mercy in Christ crucified. In embracing Christ, we justify the counsel of God concerning our salvation.

Do consider what a loving God we have, who would not be so much in love with his only Son as to keep him to himself when we needed him; a God that accounts himself most glorious in those attributes that are most for our comfort. He accounts himself glorious not so much for his wisdom, for his power or for his justice, as for his mercy and grace, for his *philanthropia*, his love of man. Shall we not therefore be even inflamed with a desire to gratify him, who has joined his glory with our salvation; who accounts himself glorious in his mercy above all other attributes? Shall the angels – who do not have that benefit by Christ as we have – shall they in our behalf, out of love to us and zeal to God's glory, sing from heaven, 'Glory to God on high'? And shall we who reap the crop be so dead and frozen-hearted as not to acknowledge this glory of God breaking out in the gospel, the glory of his mercy and rich grace?

The apostle is so full when he comes to his theme that he cannot speak without words of amplification and enlargement, once calling it 'rich grace' (*Eph.* 1:7), another time standing in admiration: 'Oh the depth of the riches . . . ' (*Rom.* 11:33). What deserves admiration but glorious things? The best testimony that can be given of glorious things is when we admire them. Now is there anything else so admirable about which we could say, 'Oh the height and depth', as we may of the love of God in Christ? Here are all the dimensions of unparalleled glory: height, and breadth, and depth. I beseech you, let us often stand in admiration of the love of God to us in Christ. 'So God loved the world' (*John* 3:16) – *so*. How? We cannot tell how. 'So' is beyond all expression. The Scripture itself is at a stand for words.

Oh base nature, that we are dazzled by anything but that which we should most admire. How few of us spend our thoughts this way, considering God's wonderful and admirable mercy and grace in Christ, when there is no object in the world so sweet and comforting as this. The very angels desire to pry into the mystery of our salvation by Christ. They are mere students. The cherubim were set upon the mercy seat having a counterview, one upon another, implying a kind of admiration. They pry into the secrets of God's love in governing his people and bringing them to heaven. Shall they do it, and shall not we study and admire these things, that God may have the glory? God made all for his glory, and 'the wicked for the day of wrath', as Solomon says (*Prov.* 16:4).

And has he not now made all for his glory? Is not the new creature more for his glory than the old creature? If we will prove that we are new creatures, let us seek to glorify God in every way, not in word alone, but in heart admiring him, and in life conversing with him.

And to glorify God in deed, let us glory in God's love, for we must glory in this glory. Nature is glorious of itself, yet vainglorious. But do you wish to glory without vanity? Go out of yourselves and see what you are in Christ, in the grace and mercy and free love of God, who called us out from the rest of mankind. There you may glory safely over sin and death and hell. For being justified freely from your sins, you can think of death, of the damnation of others, of hell, without fear. 'God forbid', says St Paul, 'that I should glory in anything, but in the cross of Christ' (*Gal.* 6:14); that is, in the mercy of God appointing such a means for satisfaction. 'Let not the wise man glory in his wisdom, nor the strong man glory in his strength' (*Jer.* 9:23). There is a danger in such glorying. It is subject to a curse. But if a man will glory, let him 'glory in the Lord'.

Use 2. If God accounts his mercy and love in Christ his special glory, shall we think that God will admit of any partner with Christ in the matter of salvation?

If, as the psalmist says, 'he made us, and not we ourselves' (*Psa.* 100:3), shall we think that we have a hand in making ourselves again? Will God allow his glory to be encroached upon by intercessions of saints' merits, and satisfaction, and free will? Grace is not glorious if we add the least thing of our own to it. We cannot make a hair of our head or the grass that we trample upon, but there must be a glory and power of God in it. And can we bring ourselves to heaven? Away with 'Hail, Mary, full of grace!' The right interpretation is 'Hail, Mary, freely beloved!' And those who attribute power and grace and favour to her in saying, 'O beseech thy Son,' and so on, are taking away that in which God and Christ will be glorified and attributing it to his mother and other creatures. I only touch on this to bring us to loathe and detest religion which sets the creature against that in which above all God will be glorified.

Use 3. Let us sustain ourselves, when we walk in darkness, by considering the gloriousness of God's mercy in Jesus Christ.

It is no less mercy than glorious mercy that will satisfy us when our conscience is distressed; and if this will not, what will? Let Satan join with conscience to aggravate our sins as much as he can. But set this glorious mercy against all our worst sins – they are sins of a finite creature. But here is infinite mercy, triumphing and rejoicing over justice, having won the victory over it. Oh, when the time of temptation comes, and the hour of death, and conflict with conscience, and all together that may discourage, Satan will bestir himself. He is cunning and eloquent and will focus completely upon sin, especially in the time of despair. But you, be as cunning to focus upon mercy, glorious mercy. If God were glorious in all other attributes, and not in mercy, what would become of us? The glory of other attributes without mercy leads us to despair: glory in wisdom to find us out, glory in justice to deal with us in rigour. These fill us with dread, but what sweetens all other attributes is his mercy.

What a comfort this is to sinful man, that in casting himself upon Christ and upon God's mercy in Christ, he yields glory to God; that God has joined his glory with our special good; that here is a sweet concurrence between the chief end and the highest good of man! The last end of man is the glory of God, for that is the point from which all came (for he made all for his glory) and in which all ends; so is the chief good.

[80]

And so it is vain for some to think, 'Oh, we must not look to our own salvation so much; this is self-love.' That is true if we sever the consideration of the glory of God's mercy and goodness from it. But we must see that both of these wrapped and indissolubly knit together in our salvation is to God's glory. We hinder God's glory if we do not believe his mercy in Christ to us. So we wrong both ourselves and him. And we wrong him not in a lesser attribute, but in his mercy and goodness, in which he has appointed to glorify himself most of all.

And so I beseech you, let us yield to him the glory of his mercy, and let us think that when we sin we cannot glorify him more than to have recourse to his mercy. When Satan tempts us to run from God and discourages us, as he will do at such times, then keep this in mind: God has set himself to be glorious in mercy above all other attributes. And as this is the primary moving attribute that stirs up all the rest, God will account himself honoured if we have recourse to him. Let this thought be as a city of refuge. When the avenger of blood follows you, flee immediately to this sanctuary. Think: Let me not deny myself comfort and God glory both at once. 'Where sin abounds, grace abounds much more' (*Rom.* 5:20). Though sins after conversion stain our profession more than sins before conversion, go still to the glorious mercy of God. To seventy times seventy times, there is yet mercy. We beseech you be reconciled, said St Paul to the Corinthians, when they were in the state of grace and already had their pardon. Let us never be discouraged from going to Christ.

'Oh, but I have offended often and grievously.' What does the prophet say? 'My thoughts are not as your thoughts but are as high as the heavens are above the earth' (*Isa.* 55:8–9). With men, offences often cause permanent alienation, but with God this is not so. As often as we have spirit to go to God for mercy and spread our sins before him with broken and humble hearts, we may receive pardon. Compare Exodus 33 and 34. Moses had desired to see the face of God. There was some little curiosity perhaps in it. God told him that none could see him and live. To see the face of God must be reserved for heaven; we are not fit for that sight. But in the next chapter, he shows himself to Moses. And how does he show himself and his glory to Moses? 'The Lord, the Lord, gracious, merciful, long-suffering', clothed all in sweet attributes. He will be known by those names.

Now then, if we would know the name of God and see God as he is pleased and delighted to reveal himself to us, let us know him by those names that he proclaims there, showing that the glory of the Lord in the gospel especially shines in mercy. And, as I said before, it must be glorious mercy that can satisfy a distressed conscience. In the time of ease and peace we think a little mercy will serve the turn; but when conscience is once awaked, it must be glorious and infinite mercy that allays it.

If you find your conscience at all wounded with any sin, do not hold back from God any longer. Come and yield, lay down your weapons; there is mercy ready. The Lord is glorious in his mercy in Jesus Christ. It is a victorious triumphing mercy over all sin and unworthiness whatever. Look upon God in the face of Jesus Christ. 'God, who commanded light to shine out of darkness, has shined in our hearts, to give us the light of the knowledge of God, in the face of Jesus Christ' (*2 Cor.* 4:6). In the face of Christ God is lovely. Loveliness and excellency are in the face more than in all other parts of the body.

We are never in the condition in which we ought to

be, unless grace is glory to us. And when is grace glory to a sinner? Oh, when he feels the weight and burden of his sin and languishing desires. Oh, that I might have a drop of mercy! Then grace is glory, not only in God's esteem, but in the eye of the sinner. Indeed, we are never soundly humbled till grace is glory in our esteem; that is, until it appears excellent and victorious. I beseech you to remember this. You may have to make use of it in the time of desertion.

'AS IN A GLASS'

How is this grace of God in Christ conveyed to us yet nearer? By the gospel. The gospel is the 'good word of God' (*Heb.* 6:5). It reveals the good God to us, and the good Christ. It is a sweet word. Christ could do us no good without the Word, if there were not an obligation, a covenant made between God and us, the foundation of which covenant is the satisfaction of Christ. If there were not promises built upon the covenant of grace, by which God has made himself a debtor, what claim could a sinful soul have to Christ and to God's mercy? But God has bound himself in his Word. The grace of God shines in Christ, and all that is in Christ is conveyed to us by the Word, by the promise. The gospel then is a sweet word.

You know that promise that begets all others, 'the seed of the woman' (*Gen.* 3:15). That repealed the curse and conveyed the mercy of God in Christ to Adam. So all the sweet and gracious promises have their source in that. All meet in Christ as in a centre; all are made for him and in him; he is the sum of all the promises. All the good things we have are parcels of Christ. Christ is the Word of the Father, who reveals all from the bosom of his Father. Therefore he is named 'the Word'.

The gospel is the Word from him. Christ was revealed to the apostles, and from the apostles to us, to the end of the world by his Spirit accompanying the ordinance. So the mirror in which we see the glorious mercy of God is first Christ. God shines in him, and then there is another glass in which Christ is revealed, the glass of the gospel. It pleases God to condescend to stoop to us poor sinners, to reveal his glory, the glory of his mercy, fitly and suitably in a Saviour, God-man, God incarnate, God our brother, God our kinsman; and to do it all yet more familiarly, to reveal it in a word. And then he ordained a ministry together with the Word to lay open the riches of Christ – for it is not the gospel considered alone, but the gospel unfolded by the ministry.

Christ is the great ordinance of God for our salvation. The gospel is the great ordinance of God, to lay open 'the unsearchable riches of Christ' (*Eph.* 3:8). The case of this jewel, the treasury of his treasure, the storehouse of the grace and love and mercy of God, is Christ. And Christ and all good things are stored in the gospel; that is the rich mine. And the ministry of the gospel lays open that mine to the people.

But God goes yet further. Along with the ministry, he gives his Holy Spirit. It is the ministry of the Spirit, that however many there are who are not called and converted in the gospel, still the Spirit of God is beforehand with them. And there are none under the gospel except those to whom the Spirit gives sweet stirrings. He knocks at their hearts, he attracts and persuades them. And if they do not yield, it is because of the rebellion of their hearts. More grace of the Spirit is offered than is accepted, so that the mouths of men shall be stopped. Thus God descends, and Christ, and grace, the gospel, the ministry, the Spirit, all by way of love to us, that we may do all in a way of love to God again.

The gospel is the mirror, the glass, in which we see this glory. And Christ indeed in a sense is the glass, for seeing God without Christ is a terrifying sight. But in the glass, Christ, we can see God as we see the sun in the water. If we cannot see the sun, which is only a creature, in its glory, how could we see God himself but in a glass? We must see him in Christ, so the sight of him is comforting. And in the dispensing of the gospel, especially in the preaching and unfolding of the Word, the riches of God in Christ are unfolded; and not only unfolded, but the Spirit conveys its sense, assurance, and persuasion to us.

There is such a connection between the evangelical truth of God and Jesus Christ that they both have one name (*Logos* and *Aletheia*, Word and Truth), to show us that as we will be partakers of Christ, so it must be of Christ as he is revealed in the gospel, and not in ideas of our own. The Word is truth, and Christ is truth; they have the same name. There could be ever so much mercy and love in God; but if it were concealed from us so that we had nothing to plead and no title to it by a revelation of it in his will, the Word and the sacraments (for the Word and sacraments make one whole; the one is the evidence, the other the seal), what comfort could we take in it?

Now his will is in the promise, in which he not only reveals what he does or will do, but he has committed himself: If we believe, we shall not perish but have life (*John* 3:15); and, Come unto me (*Matt.* 11:28) and be refreshed, says Christ. Everyone who thirsts, come and be satisfied (*John* 7:37). And now we may claim the performance of what he has spoken and bind him by his own Word. 'He cannot deny himself' (*2 Tim.* 2:13). So now we see him comfortingly in the mirror of the Word and sacraments.

[85]

These three go together: the glory of God; then Christ the foundation of all grace, in the covenant of grace; and finally the gospel of grace, the gospel of the kingdom, the gospel of life, which reveals the gracious face of God shining in Christ. We have communion with God through Christ and with Christ through the gospel. Therefore in the gospel 'we behold as in a glass the glory of God'.

This suits our condition while we are here below. We cannot see divine things any other way but in a glass. The sight of God that we shall have in heaven, directly, without the Word and sacraments, is of a higher nature, when our natures shall be perfect. While we live here we cannot see God but in Christ; and we cannot see him but in the Word and sacraments. Such is the imperfection of our sight, and such is the lustre and glory of the object, the glory of God. God said to Moses, 'None can see me and live.' He meant, 'None can see me as I am, none can see me directly, and live.'

If we would see God and the glory of God directly, without a glass, it must be in heaven. We must die first and pass through death to see God face to face more familiarly than we can now. Then God will represent himself for our happiness – though not simply as he is, for he is infinite; and how could finite comprehend infinite? We shall apprehend him, but not comprehend him. While we are on earth, then, we must be content to see him in a glass, which is the gospel, especially unfolded.

Now the word 'glass', in which we see the glory of God, implies both a perfection and some imperfection.

It implies *perfection,* because it is like a clear crystal glass in comparison with the glass that was before. Those under the law saw Christ in a glass of ceremonies. And, as I said before, there is a difference between seeing one's face in water and seeing it in a crystal mirror. So the word implies perfection with regard to the former state.

It implies *imperfection* with regard to heaven, for there we shall not see in a glass. Sight in a mirror is imperfect, though more perfect than seeing in water. From experience we know that a reflection weakens the image; and the more reflections, the weaker the image. When we see the sun on the wall, it is weaker than the light of the sun itself. And when it reflects upon another wall, the third reflection is weaker still. When a man sees his face in a glass, it is a weaker representation than seeing face to face. So here all sight by glass is not as powerful as the sight and knowledge which is face to face in heaven.

That is the reason that St James says that he who sees his face in a glass is likely to forget (*James* 1:24). Why can a man not remember himself when he sees his face in a glass, as well as he can remember another man's face? Because he sees himself only by reflection. It is a weaker presentation, and the memory and apprehension of it is weaker. When he sees another face to face, he remembers him longer because the representation is more lively. It is not a reflection, but face to face.

So while we are here our sight of God is imperfect, as in a glass. It is nothing compared with seeing face to face, without the Word and sacraments or any other medium. We shall know this sight better when we are there; we cannot now discover it. It is a part of heaven to know what apprehensions we shall have of God there. But surely it is more excellent than that which is here. The word 'glass', then, implies imperfection.

We consist of body and soul in this world, and our souls are much confined and tied to our senses. Imagination sets forth to the soul greater things than the senses. So God helps the soul by outward things that work upon the senses. The senses work upon the imagination, and so things pass into the soul. God's manner of dealing is suited to the nature he has created us in. By using the Word and sacraments and such things, he makes impressions upon the very soul itself.

And this indeed, by the way, makes spiritual things so difficult as they often are, because we are too enthralled to imagination and sense and cannot separate our minds from outward tangible things and raise them to spiritual things. There are some who all their lives spend their time in the bark of the Scriptures; and they are better than some others who are all for notions and such things that suit the imagination, and who never come to know the spirit of the Scriptures, but rest in outward things, in languages and tongues, and such. In contrast, these things lead further, or else they are not complete. The Scripture is but a glass, to see some excellencies in it.

One purpose for using a glass is to help weakness of sight against the brightness of an object. When sight is weak and the object brilliant, then a glass is used, or some polished and clear body. We cannot look at the sun; the eye is weak, and the sun is glorious. So we look at the sun in water, as in an eclipse. If a man would judge an eclipse he must not look at the sun, but see it in water. In the same way, the glory of God in himself is too glorious an object; our eyes are too weak. How does God help it? He helps it by a glass, by 'God manifest in the flesh' (*1 Tim.* 3:16), and by the Word and sacraments by which we come to have communion with Christ.

Now that we are to receive the sacrament, think of the sacraments as glasses in which we see the glory of the love and mercy of God in Christ. If we consider the bread alone, and not as representing better things, what is it? And the wine alone, as it does not represent better things, what is it but an ordinary poor thing? Oh, but take them as glasses, as things that convey to the soul and represent things more excellent than themselves, and they are glorious ordinances. Take a glass as a glass, it is a poor thing; but take the glasses as they represent more excellent things than themselves, and they are of excellent use. Bread and wine must not be taken as naked elements, but as they represent and convey something more excellent: that is, Christ and all his benefits, the love and mercy and grace of God in Christ.

Therefore I beseech you now, when you are to receive the sacrament, let your minds be more occupied than your senses. When you take the bread, think of the body of Christ broken; and when you think of uniting the bread into one substance, think of Christ and you made one. When the wine is poured out, think of the blood of Christ poured out for sin. When you think of the refreshing by the wine, think of the refreshing of your spirits and souls by the love of God in Christ, and of the love of Christ that did not spare his blood for your soul's good. How Christ crucified and his shedding of blood refreshes the guilty soul, as wine refreshes the weak spirits! So consider the sacraments as glasses in which better things are presented, and let your minds as well as your senses be occupied, and then you shall be fit receivers.

'WE BEHOLD'

When God made the world, this glorious frame of the creatures and all their excellencies, he created light to reveal itself and all other excellencies. Light is a glorious thing. It reveals itself. It goes with a majesty and reveals all other things, good and bad. And together with light,

God created sight and other senses in man, to apprehend the excellency of the creation. What would all these good creations be, the sun, and moon, and stars, and glory of the earth, if there were not light to reveal and sight to apprehend it by? And if that is so in this outward creation of the old heavens and old earth that must be consumed with fire – is it not much more so in the new creation? There is excellent glory, marvellous glory, wondrous grace in Christ. Must there be light, and must not there be an eye to discover this? Surely there must. Therefore it is said here, 'We behold.'

God puts a spiritual eye by his Spirit into all true believers, by which they behold this excellent glory, this glorious grace, that God may have the glory, and we the comfort. Those are the two main ends. God intends his own glory and our salvation. There must be a 'beholding'. How should he have glory and we comfort, unless all were conveyed by spiritual sight? Well then, the Spirit creates and works in us spiritual senses. With spiritual life there are spiritual senses, sight, and taste, and feeling. Sight is here put for all: 'We behold.'

We see God in several ways:

We see God *in his creation*, for 'the heavens declare the glory of God'. They are a book in folio. There God is laid open in his creation. That is a pleasing sight. But what is this compared to knowing him in his will to us, what he means to us? The creatures do not know what he means to us.

We see God *in his will, and in his Word and promises*. There we see what he is, his grace revealed in Christ, what his good will is to us, and what he wills from us. There we see him as a spouse sees her husband in a loving letter which concerns herself. We see him as the heir sees a deed made to him with an inheritance. It is not a sight only, but a sight with feeling and discovery of a favour. So the sight in the Word and sacraments is higher than that in the created universe.

Christ was seen when he was in the flesh. When he was covered with the veil of our flesh upon earth, that was a sweet sight. Abraham desired to see it (*John* 8:56); and Simeon, when he saw it, was willing to depart (*Luke* 2:29). Yet this outward sight is nothing without an inward sight of faith.

We see *by faith*, and other sights are to no purpose without this, the sight of God shining in Christ. And it will be perfected in heaven, in the sight of glory, when we shall see him as he is.

There is comfort in all these sights of God in his Word and works. It was glorious to see him in his bodily presence, and by faith to see the face of God shining in Christ. Oh, but what is all this to the sight of him hereafter in glory!

Now the 'beholding' meant here is the beholding of faith, in the ordinances, in the Word and sacraments. We all 'behold', as in the glass of the Word and sacraments, by the eye of faith. Faith is expressed by beholding, by knowledge. For indeed, faith is knowledge applied; faith includes knowledge. What is faith, but to know God and Christ and the promises as mine? Christ in the sacrament is mine as truly as the outward things are mine; knowledge applied is faith. 'We behold.'

The knowledge of the mind is compared to the eye of the body. Knowledge and faith are compared to seeing and beholding, for these reasons:

Sight is *the noblest and most glorious sense*. It is also the quickest, for in a moment sight apprehends its object in the highest heavens. So it is with faith. It is the noblest sight of all. And it is as quick as sight; for faith is that eagle in the cloud. It breaks through all and sees in a moment Christ in heaven; it looks backward and sees

Christ upon the cross; it looks forward and sees Christ to come in glory. Faith is so quick a grace that it presents things past, things above and things to come – all in a moment, so quick is this eagle-eye of faith.

Sight is *the broadest sense*. We can see almost the whole hemisphere at one view. That a little thing in the eye should apprehend so much in a moment! As it is quick in apprehension, so it is large in comprehension.

Sight is *the surest sense*, more sure than hearing, and that is why the divine act of knowledge is compared to seeing. Believing is compared to beholding. When faith looks upon God in the glass of the Word and promises, it is as certain as the object itself. Now, how certain is the object? The mercy and love of God in Christ, who is truth itself, is most certain.

Sight is *the sense that works most upon the soul*; what the body sees affects and moves the soul. It works upon the affections most. Desire and love rise out of sight. That is why the knowledge that stirs up the affections and works upon the heart is compared to sight. It affects us marvellously: corresponding to our faith, we love, and joy, and delight. Knowledge alters the whole man.

We see, then, why this spiritual beholding is compared to outward sight: it is a most noble spiritual act of the soul, and it is most certain and sure. 'Faith is the evidence of things not seen' (*Heb.* 11:1), and it works upon the heart and soul. We should labour to clear the eye of the soul, that we may behold the glory of God in the glass of the gospel.

Question. How shall we make the eye of our souls fit to behold the glory of God?

Answer 1. We must fix the eye of the soul; fix our meditation upon the glory of God and the excellency of Christ. A moving, rolling eye sees nothing. We must set some time apart to fix our meditations upon the excellent things in the gospel.

Answer 2. We must also labour to have both inward and outward hindrances removed.

We must labour that the soul be cleansed from all carnal and base passions and desires. Only a spiritual soul can ever behold spiritual things. The physical eye cannot apprehend rational things, nor the rational eye behold spiritual things. There must be a spiritual eye, and there must be some proportion between the soul and spiritual things before the soul can behold them. As the soul must be fixed upon these meditations, so the Spirit of God must sanctify and purge the soul.

Sight is also hindered from without by dust in the eyes, clouds and such things. Satan uses the dust of the world to hinder the sight of the soul from beholding the glory of God in the gospel. The apostle says in the next chapter that the god of this world blinds the eyes of men. 'If the gospel be hid, it is hid to them that are lost', that perish, 'in whom the god of this world has blinded the minds of them that believe not, lest the light of the glorious gospel of Christ should shine unto them' (*2 Cor.* 4:3–4). Take heed of fixing our souls upon the dust of the world, upon things here below. We do not see Christ, and God in Christ, by fixing the soul upon base things below. Let us take care that our souls are inwardly cleansed and fixed upon spiritual things, and then we shall better behold the glory of God shining in the gospel.

And we should preserve this sight of faith by hearing. Hearing begets seeing in religion. Death came in by the ear at the beginning, when Adam listened to the serpent that he should not have listened to. So life, too, comes in by the ear. We hear, and then we see: 'As we have heard, so have we seen,' says the psalm (*Psa.* 48:8). It is also true in religion; most of our sight comes by hearing, which is the sense of learning. God has made it so. We should therefore behold all we can the glory of the Lord in the glass of the Word; and to that end hear much.

You will ask me, What is the best glass of all to see and know Christ in? To behold Christ in the glass of the Word, with a spirit of faith – that is the best picture and representation that can be! The best picture to see Christ in is the Word and sacraments. And the best eye to see him with is the eye of faith in the Word and sacraments. In Galatians 3:1 St Paul says: 'O foolish Galatians, before whom Christ has been painted and crucified!' How was he painted? By the preaching of Christ crucified in the gospel, and the riches of Christ in the gospel, and in the sacraments laid open.

'WITH OPEN FACE'

The manner of this beholding is 'with open face'. Before we can behold the glory of God, a double veil must be taken away: the veil of slavery, and the veil of obscurity; the veil of ignorance and infidelity within, and the veil of the things themselves. The inward veil is taken away by the Spirit of God illuminating our understanding and giving us a spirit of faith. The veil of obscurity is taken away by the teaching and ministry of the gospel, which helps us to know the meaning of the Scriptures.

In these glorious times of the gospel, both the veils are taken away, that we may behold without hindrance the glory of God shining in the gospel, for now we enjoy the ministry of the Spirit. The Spirit is effectual to shine in our hearts. And we also have the gifts of men, outward gifts, by which the things themselves are unfolded and the veil of ignorance is taken away. There can be no seeing if the things themselves are dark; or if they are light but there is no sight within; or if there is sight but the sight is veiled. But now God takes away all these veils from his elect; he shines inwardly and gives outward light by the help of means.

Yet while we live here, there is always some obscurity and darkness, for the veil of the Scriptures is not completely taken away; neither is the veil of ignorance and infidelity. There remain some ignorance, infidelity, and hardness of heart. Yet the veils are taken away here in great measure, and shall little by little be further taken away, till we see God face to face in heaven.

Veils had two uses in the Jewish state. They indicated subjection, and so were worn by women. They also indicated obscurity, to hinder the overwhelming lustre of the glorious. So Moses put a veil on his face when he came down from the mount.

Now in Christ Jesus in the gospel, both these veils are taken away in some respects. The veil of subjection and slavery is taken away because the Spirit of Christ works liberty. We now serve God as sons and no longer as servants. A spouse-like, filial subjection remains, but we are freed from servile subjection. And the veil that hid the things is taken away, too. So now 'with open face we behold the glory of the Lord'. The things themselves, Christ and the gracious promises of grace and glory and comfort, are now clearly laid open without any veil.

Then why do we not see them? Because there is a veil over our hearts. The more shame for us, that when these things are unveiled we should have a veil of ignorance and unbelief upon our hearts. If any do not believe, it is because 'the god of this world has blinded their eyes' (*2 Cor.* 4:4). Where the means of salvation are, and where Christ is laid open in the means, if men do not believe, the fault is not in the things themselves. The fault is in us. A cloud of ignorance and unbelief keeps the heart from beholding the glory of the mercy of God in Christ.

We see the glory of God with boldness in the gospel. We have boldness and access to God through Christ by the Spirit, as St Paul teaches (*Eph.* 3:12, *Heb.* 10:19). Christ by his Spirit takes us by the hand and leads us to his Father. God is not now terrifying to us; but in Christ, God's nature is fatherly and sweet to us.

We may boldly lay open our souls in prayer and bring all our complaints before him as to a Father. We do not come as malefactors to a judge or as slaves to a lord, but as children to a father, as a wife to her spouse. The gospel by shining upon us takes away a spirit of fear and bondage. The more we see Christ, and the more love, the less fear. The more we see the grace of God in Christ, the spirit of fear is diminished and replaced by a spirit of love and boldness. Grace presents to us in Christ full satisfaction to divine justice. When we offer Christ to the Father whom he has sent and sealed for us, God cannot refuse a Saviour of his own sending, sealing and appointing. It is a marvellous privilege that we see God clearly in the gospel, with open faces, with a spirit of boldness, the veil of ignorance being taken away.

For the sight of God to a conscience that is natural and not convinced of the mercy of God by the Spirit is a terrifying sight. A guilty conscience cannot see a man without trembling. It cannot see a judge without trembling. And will not the guilty soul, that trembles at the sight of a man, flee the more from the face of God? What is so contrary as the nature of God to the nature of man out of Christ – the unholy, impure, and unclean nature of man, to the pure, holy nature of God? If Christ had not taken our nature and sanctified it in himself, and satisfied justice in it, what boldness could this unclean nature of ours have to go to the holy God? Let us, I beseech you, be wrapped up in admiration of the singular love of God to us, especially in these days of the gospel, in which we see in a clear glass the love of God in Christ, and with open face we may go boldly to God.

Sometimes when the soul is bold in sin, it weakens boldness and faith and makes us look upon the correction that our sins deserve. For however we may behold his glorious face in Christ, if we sin against conscience, God will hide himself, Christ will hide his face and hide the promises, and leave us to terrors of conscience. And the soul sees not God's gracious face in Christ, but the correction that our sin deserves. God has power over the soul and makes the soul apprehend what he will. And he presents to a bold soul that runs into sin what it deserves: hell for the present. There is no terror that compares to the terror of a Christian that is bold in sin, till God again shines upon him in his grace. Sins against conscience weaken faith, so that we cannot go so boldly to God. Those who say when they sin against conscience, that all the cause of their grief is that they do not conceive the free mercy of God, are ignorant of God's ways. God is wise, and though he pardons sin, as sin is pardoned in heaven, we shall never be pardoned in conscience till God has made the conscience sting for it. And God will let wrath into our conscience, and our faith shall falter. It will tremble and quake till we have humbled ourselves before God.

How shall we recover ourselves after our boldness and sweet familiarity with God has been interrupted by sin?
Surely, to know that our sins are pardonable in Christ, that God is an everlasting Father, and that the covenant of grace is everlasting – the awareness of mercy must work our hearts to grief and shame. That is certain. Notice in the gospel: 'Come unto me, all ye that are

weary and heavy laden' (*Matt.* 11:28). He calls us when we find our consciences afflicted and tormented. 'He came to save that which was lost' (*Matt.* 18:11). By the blessed power of the Spirit, the blood of Christ is as a fountain for Judah and Jerusalem to wash in (*Zech.* 13:1), and the 'blood of Christ purges us from sin' (*1 John* 1:7). Christ tells us to ask pardon for daily trespasses (*Matt.* 6:12). Daily, therefore, perceive goodness in God still, an everlasting current of mercy. This must work in us grief and shame, and recover and strengthen our faith again. And God's children, after breaches, emerge stronger than they ever were before; but this only by the way.

We see here how God's glorious grace is conveyed to us, and how he has given us a spiritual eye to see it in the glass of the gospel. 'With open face we behold it', and we may go boldly to the throne of grace.

I beseech you, do not let this privilege of the gospel be forgotten. What is the glory of the times we live in, but God's face revealed in Christ? In the gospel, faith works in us to see God's face openly, and to come boldly with our Benjamin, our elder brother; to come with Esau's garments (*Gen.* 27:27); that is, to come with Christ, and we cannot be too bold. Remember always there must be a reverent familiarity, because God's abundant mercy is mixed with majesty. Both are mixed together. So our approach to him must be loving and familiar, as he is full of mercy. But then he has majesty. A reverent familiarity is fit for a father, and for so gracious and sweet a God. That is why we see those phrases in the Scriptures, 'We go boldly', and cry, 'Abba, Father' (*Rom.* 8:15). Father is a word of reverence. We go boldly to God in Christ and open our wants as to a father, with love and reverence; as it is said here, 'with open face'. Let us not forget this privilege.

'WE ALL'

In Moses' time, he went alone onto the mount and saw God. But now it is 'we all', that is Jews and Gentiles, wherever the gospel is preached. You see that the church is enlarged by the coming of Christ. It was a comfort to St Paul and to all good Christians to think of the enlargement of the church by taking in the Gentiles, and it will be a comfort to think of the enlarging of the church by taking in the Jews again. In religion, the more the better.

Why is it a privilege for many, why 'we all'? Because in matters of grace and glory there is no envy at all. All may share without prejudice. Here on earth not all can be kings, nor can all be great men, because the more one has the less another has. But in Christ and in religion, all may have grace. God respects all as one, and one, as if there were no one else. And every one entirely enjoys Christ, as if there were no others. There is no envy, as I said, in grace and glory, where all may share alike. That is why it is always comforting to think of community in religion; it is joined with comfort.

And indeed, it is also comforting to see a communion of many in one. For what is the mystical body of Christ Jesus but many members joined in one body, under one gracious and glorious head? A divided and disunited body is deformed. That is what the devil rules in: divide and rule. It is fit for the devil. But God and Christ rule in union. The same Spirit of God that knits the members to the head by faith knits the members to one another in love; and all grace is derived from the head to the members, as they are united to the body. So far as there is disunion no grace is conveyed from the head; for the body grows up under one head.

Then let us labour to cherish union and hate division.

No one gains by disunion but the devil himself. His policy is always to make any breach greater. But the more that join together in the blessed mysteries of the gospel, the more comfort and the more glory there is. When all live and join together in the holy things of God, and in sweet love toward one another, it is the glory of that place and society and state.

By all means labour for union, especially now that we are to take the communion, which is a seal of our communion with Christ by faith and with one another. By love let us labour to bring our hearts to a holy communion.

6: *Our Conformity to the Image of Christ*

'. . . and are changed into the same image, from glory to glory, as by the Spirit of the Lord.'

I showed before how man's happiness stands partly in communion with God, and partly in his conformity and likeness to God. This conformity is shown as springing from communion – 'We all behold the glory of God.' Now, reconciled in Jesus Christ, that beholding works conformity.

In these words we see that change is necessary, and in this change there must be a pattern of conformity. We are changed into the image of Christ, who is the prototype, the first idea of all perfection.

We also see how this change to the image of Christ is brought about: it is by beholding the glory of Christ in the gospel. God's mercy in Christ is not only an object of delight, but it is a powerful object that influences and transforms the soul.

The state of man after this change is a glorious condition, and it is also a growing condition: 'We are changed from glory to glory' till the soul is filled 'with all the fullness of God', as the apostle says (*Eph.* 3:19).

These things follow one another. We begin with the first.

'AND ARE CHANGED'

We must be changed from the state in which we are, as Christ tells Nicodemus (*John* 3:7), and such a change as a new birth. It must be all new, just as a bell that has even one crack must be newly moulded and recast. It is the same with the soul: if there is one flaw or crack, it is nothing and must be cast and moulded anew. All is out of tune; we must be set in tune again. Before the soul can make any sweet harmony in the ears of God, there must be a change. There is no coming to heaven without a change. This is so basic to religion – except we be born anew we cannot enter into heaven (*John* 3:3) – that I press the point only to make clear from evidence of reason the necessity of a change in the whole person.

a) First, we are in a state contrary to grace and to God. We are dead. There must be life in us before we come to heaven. We are enemies and must be made friends. How shall we be fit for communion with God, in whom our happiness lies, without conformity? Communion is between friends. Before those opposed to each other can be friends, there must be an alteration; and this alteration must be either on God's part, or on ours.

Now, who must change? God, who is unchangeable, or we, who are corrupt and changeable? God will not change. There is no reason he should. He is goodness itself, his perfection unique. There is not a shadow of change in God. Therefore, when there is a difference between God and us, the change must be on our part. We must be changed in the spirit of our minds (*Rom.* 12:2). We must be wholly moulded anew. Where there is a condition so opposite as is the frame of our hearts toward God, he being holiness and we a mass and lump of sin, there must be a change.

In the gospel God intends to bring us near himself, and Christ's end is to bring us to God (*1 Pet.* 3:18). All the gospel is to bring us back to God from whom we fell. Now our nature, as I said, is defiled and unholy, and we

[102]

cannot be friends with God till there is some likeness to him. Our natures must in some measure be suitable to the sweet and holy and pure nature of God. We enter into a covenant with God, in the covenant of grace – and how can we maintain the covenant of grace, without some likeness to God and Christ? Again, there must be a change, and this change must be on our part. On a musical instrument, those strings that are out of tune are adjusted to those that are in tune. In the same way, it is we who must alter, and not God. God is always unchangeable, like himself in his love. And it is our comfort that he is so unchangeable in his mercy and holiness and justice.

Flesh and blood as it is, that is, the corrupted nature of man, cannot enter into heaven (*1 Cor.* 15:50). We must have new judgements and new desires, new esteem, new affections, new joys and delights, new company. The whole frame and bent of the soul must be new. The face of the soul must look altogether another way. Whereas before it looked to the world, to things below, now it must look to God and heaven. Those still in their natural state, who feel no change in themselves, are not in the state of grace, for there must be a change.

And it is a double change, real and gradual. The real change is from ill to good, from the state of nature to a state of grace. This happens at our first conversion, when God puts the first form and stamp upon us. The gradual change is from better to better, from glory to glory.

b) We all expect glory in heaven. But how can we reach that unless we are made fit for it? The church is the fitting place for glory. We enter into heaven in the church here. We are hewn and squared here. If we are not holy here, we shall never enter into heaven. The change must begin here if ever it is to be perfected in heaven. No unclean thing shall come there (*Rev.* 21:27). As soon as Satan, an angel of light, sinned, he was tumbled out of heaven. It will allow no unclean thing; no unclean thing shall ever come there again. Our nature must be altered suitable to that place and glorious condition, before we go to heaven. Unless we are new born, we cannot enter into the kingdom of God.

But this is forgotten. Men trust to the grace and mercy of God, but do not look for a change; and this prevents many from embracing the whole truth of the gospel and from knowing Christ as the truth is in him. They hear that they must be changed, and they are unwilling. They believe that God is merciful, and that Christ died, and so on. They snatch enough of the gospel to build them up in self-love and think all is well. But when they see the kind of grace that must teach them to 'deny ungodliness and worldly lusts' (*Titus* 2:12), and the grace that must alter them, this they cannot endure. They are content to go to heaven if they may have it in a way to hell, in maintaining their corruptions, being proud and covetous and worldly as they are. This must not be. There must of necessity be a change.

c) The soul that truly desires mercy and favour always desires power against sin. Pardon and power go together, both in God's gift and in the desire of a Christian's soul. There is no Christian soul that does not desire the grace of sanctification to change him as much as the grace of pardon. He looks upon corruption and sin as the vilest thing in the world, and upon grace and the new creature as the best thing in the world. There is no one changed who does not desire also sanctification.

Some weak notions would place all the change in justification. They separate Christ's offices, as if he were all priest but not a governing king; or as if he were righteousness but not sanctification; or as if he had merit to die for us and to give us his righteousness, but no efficacy to change our natures; or as if in the covenant of grace God only forgave our sins but did not write his law in our hearts. But in the covenant of grace he does both. Where God makes a combination, we must not break it. Efficacy and merit, justification and sanctification, water and blood, go together. There must be a change.

d) Actions correspond to powers and abilities, and no holy action can come from an unchanged ability. A change in the soul's faculties must precede a change in life and conduct.

In nature, there is first the form, living, and being of a thing; then there are powers and, finally, actions issuing from the powers. In nature we live, and we have the power to move; being and moving go together. So if we have a being in grace, we have a power to move. In the life of grace and sanctification there is an ability to believe in God, to be holy, and to love God; and then the actions of love spring from that power. Consider, then, the necessity of a change of the inward man, of the powers of the soul. Can the eye see without a power of seeing? or the ear hear without a faculty of hearing? Can the soul perform sanctified actions without a sanctified power? It is impossible.

And the change is especially in the will, which some would say is not touched. They would say the will is free and would give grace no more credit than necessary. But grace works upon the will most of all. For the bent and desires of the will carry the whole man with it. If the choice, and bent, and bias are the right way, by the Spirit, it is good. If the will is not inclined and formed to go the best way, there is no work of grace at all. Though

[105]

all grace first comes in through the understanding being enlightened, it then goes into the will. That is, it passes through the understanding into the will, and it puts a new taste and relish upon the will and affections.

You see, then, that the grace in the gospel is not mere persuasion and entreaty, but a powerful work of the Spirit entering into the soul and changing it, and altering the inclination of the will heavenward, whereas corruption of nature turns the soul downward to things below. The soul is carried up and is shut to things below. We must have great notions of the work of grace. The Scripture has great words of it. It is an alteration, a change, a new man, a new creature, a new birth.

e) Finally, whenever God calls and dignifies, he also qualifies. Princes cannot qualify those they raise, but God, whom he advances to glory, he fits and qualifies for glory. Where he bestows his mercies and favours to life everlasting, he calls to great things, and he also changes them. If Saul was changed when he came to be a king, shall we think that God will call any to the participation of his glorious mercy in Christ, in pardoning their sin and accepting them to life eternal, and yet not change them? No. Whoever he calls to glory, he changes and alters their dispositions to be fit for so glorious a condition as a Christian is called to.

Proud men do not like to hear this. It offends their former authority. 'What! I, who was accounted a wise man, now to be a fool – I, who was accounted so and so, to alter all my course and to turn the stream another way? The world will say I am mad.' I say, because grace alters everything: 'Old things are passed away, and all things are become new' (*2 Cor.* 5:17). Those that are carnal and proud cannot endure a change, because it is an affront to their reputation. But it must be so if they look for salvation.

'INTO THE SAME IMAGE'

The pattern to which we are changed is the image of Christ. It is a true rule that the first in every kind is the measure – the idea and pattern – of all the rest. Now Christ is the first, for he is the 'first-born', the 'first fruits', the 'first beloved'. He is the pattern of all the rest and the measure of all others. The nearer we come to Christ, the better we are. Christ is the best, and our nature in Christ is joined to the Godhead in one person. Therefore we are changed to the likeness of Christ – the second Adam. Before being changed, we are corrupted and depraved according to the likeness of the first Adam after his fall. If he had not fallen, we would have been born according to his likeness, that is, good and right-eous. But now, being fallen, as soon as we are planted and grafted by faith into the second Adam, we are changed into his likeness. Christ, as it were, is God's masterpiece, that is, the most excellent work and device and frame of heaven that ever was: such a mediator, to reconcile justice and mercy in bringing God and man into one person. Christ being God's masterpiece, the best and most excellent of all, he is fit to be the pattern of all excellency whatever. He is the image, the idea, the pattern of all our sanctification.

Christ, the second Adam, is the image into which we are changed. We are changed by grace, not to the image of the first Adam, but to that of the second. From him derives all good, opposite to all the ill we drew from the first Adam. From the first we drew the displeasure of God; by the death and satisfaction of the second we obtain the favour of God. By the wrath of God we drew corruption from the first Adam; in the second we have grace. From the first Adam we have death and all its attending miseries; in the second Adam we have life and all happiness, till it ends in glory. In a word, whatever ill we have in the first Adam is repaired abundantly in the second, when we are changed into his image.

When you read of the image of God in the New Testament, it must be understood of the image of God in Jesus Christ, the second Adam. This image consists in knowledge, in holiness and in righteousness. Colossians 3 and Ephesians 4 show that these were perfect in Christ, who was the image of his Father. And we must be like Christ, the second Adam, in sanctification.

We must be conformed to the image of the second Adam, and not to the first. The second Adam far excels the first; and, as I said, we must be conformed to the best image. As we have borne the image of the first, so we must bear the image of the second (*1 Cor.* 15:49).

Also, the image of God in the second Adam is more durable. All excellencies and grace are more firmly set on Christ than they ever were upon Adam. They are set upon him with such a character and stamp that they shall never be altered. When God set his image on the first Adam, it decayed and was lost by the malice of the devil because it was not set on so firmly, Adam being a man and a good man, yet changeable. But Christ is God-man. In one nature God has set such a stamp of grace on the human nature, eternally united to the Godhead, that it shall never be altered. We are renewed according to the image of God as it is stamped on Christ, not as it was stamped on the first Adam.

And that is why the state of God's children is unalterable, why being once graced they are so for ever. If God set the stamp of the Spirit of Christ on them, it is firm, as it is upon Christ. It never alters in Christ nor in those who are members of Christ, except in growth from better to better. God's children some-times deface that image by sin. But as a coin that is somewhat defaced, yet still retains the old stamp and is acknowledged for a good coin, so a Christian in all desertions, in the worst state, bears the stamp still. Though darkened by carelessness, yet after it receives a fresh stamp, it is an everlasting stamp. When once we are God's coin, we are never reprobate silver. And that is all because we are 'renewed according to the image of Christ'. Grace is firmly set in our nature in Christ, so sure that all the devils in hell cannot obliterate it. And he is the 'quickening Spirit', able to transform us to his likeness better than the first Adam was. The image of God, then, is the likeness of the second Adam, and we are changed into that.

The second Adam changes us into his own image for many reasons:

a) He is a powerful head, who changes all his members; a powerful root that changes all his branches into his own nature; a powerful husband that changes his own spouse. I say, he is a quickening Spirit and the root of all believers, as the first Adam was of us all in the natural way.

b) It is proper that brethren should be alike. We are predestinated to be conformed to Christ. He is the first among many brethren (*Rom.* 8:29). The chief brethren must be alike. Being predestinated to salvation, it was fitting we should be conformed to our elder brother, that brethren might be of one nature and disposition.

c) It is fitting, too, that the husband and wife should be of one disposition. Christ is the husband, and we are the spouse. He loved his spouse and gave himself for it, that he might purge it and make it a glorious spouse (*Eph.* 5:25-7). It is also proper that the wife should be the glory of the husband (*1 Cor.* 11:7), that is, that she should reflect the excellencies of her husband. And so the church is changed to be like Christ more and more, daily, that she might be the glory of Christ and reflect his excellencies.

God has ordained that we should be like him in a threefold degree: in suffering, in grace, and in glory. Whoever will be like him in glory must be like him in grace. But first God's election and ordaining must have their effect: the representation of the likeness of Christ in our natures.

The reason for Christ's coming was 'to destroy the works of the devil' (*1 John* 3:8), to deface all Satan's works, especially his work in us, the image of Satan in our dispositions. Every man by nature carries the image of the devil on him. He naturally opposes the truth and hates God and good things. But Christ coming to dissolve the works of the devil, he erases out this image and sets his own stamp and image upon the soul. Unless Christ changed us to his own image, he would not achieve the end for which he came.

d) The aim of Christ is for us to enter into a sweet communion with him. He will set such a stamp upon us that he may delight in us and be friends. If he did not change our natures, what accord could there be between Christ and us? But when he has altered us, he looks on us as carrying his own stamp and image.

USES

Use 1. If it is so that we are changed into the image of the second Adam, Jesus Christ, then let us labour every day more and more to study Christ, so that by beholding him we may be transformed into his likeness. *The sight of Christ is a transforming sight.*
Let us look into his disposition and his conduct as they are set forth in the Gospels; and look to his privileges, so that we may receive 'grace for grace', grace suitable to

his grace, and disposition, privilege and prerogative suitable to his, that we may be like him in every way. What was his disposition and conduct to his friends, his enemies, and the devil himself?

You see how full of love he was. What drew him from heaven to earth, and so to his cross and to his grave, but love to mankind? You see how full of goodness he was: 'He went about doing good' (*Acts* 10:38). And how much good do his words savour of, which Paul reports: 'It is more blessed to give than to receive' (*Acts* 20:35).

See how full of zeal he was! He whipped the buyers and sellers out of the temple (*John* 2:15).

He was full of goodness. It was his meat and drink to do good (*John* 4:31–34). It was as natural to him as for a fountain to stream out.

And as for his behaviour toward his friends, to those who were good, how sweet and indulgent he was.

Where there was any beginning of goodness, he encouraged it. He never sent any back again, but those who went back again of their own accord, as the young man. Christ did not send him back. He was so full of sweetness to weak Christians; indeed, he revealed himself most to the weakest. He was never more familiar with anyone than with the woman of Samaria, who was an adulteress (*John* 4:6–26); and Mary, who had been a sinner, how sweetly did he appear to her first (*John* 20:11–16). How sweet he was to sinners when they repented, how ready to forgive and pardon! See it in Peter. He never cast him in the teeth with his apostasy; he never upbraided him for it; he never so much as told him of it. He only 'looked' upon him, and afterward said, 'Lovest thou me?' (*John* 21:15).

He would not 'quench the smoking flax, nor break the bruised reed' (*Matt.* 12:20), so gentle and sweet a Saviour have we. He was sweet to those who were good in the least degree; where there was even a hint of goodness, as in the young man, he kissed and embraced him when he came and said, 'What good thing shall I do to inherit eternal life?' (*Mark* 10:17). He embraced him and made much of him. And so to the Pharisee, he said, 'Thou art not far from the kingdom of God' (*Mark* 12:34). He laboured to pull him further. He was of a winning, gaining disposition. Those who were good he loved, and he behaved so to all who might be. Shall we not labour to be of his disposition, not to set people further off, but to be of a gaining, winning nature?

See how obedient he was to his Father: 'Not as I will, but as thou wilt' (*Matt.* 26:39). Both in active and in passive obedience, in all things he looked to his Father's will, being subordinate to him. We see he prayed whole nights (*Luke* 6:12; 21:37). Wherever there is subordination, there ought to be obedience. We are subordinate to God as our Father in Christ; therefore we should labour to be obedient even to death, as Christ was. Our happiness lies in subordination. The happiness of the inferior is in subjection to the superior that may do him good.

In and of himself, how holy and heavenly he was. He took occasion of vines, of stones, of water, of sheep, and of all things to be heavenly-minded, to raise his soul upon all occasions. And when he rose from the dead and conversed with his disciples, what did he talk about? He spoke all about matters of the kingdom of heaven. So his whole disposition was heavenly and holy in himself, and he was patient in wrongs done to him. He did not return injury for injury. You see how meek he was. He was in himself full of purity and holiness and heavenliness.

And how did he behave toward his enemies? Did he call for fire from heaven when they wronged him? When his poor disciples, being more flesh than spirit, would have fire from heaven, he said, 'You know not what manner of spirit you are of' (*Luke* 9:55). He shed tears for those who shed his blood: 'O Jerusalem, Jerusalem' (*Matt.* 23:37), and who afterward crucified him. And upon the cross you see him saying of his very enemies, 'Father, forgive them, they know not what they do' (*Luke* 23:34). So then if we will be like Christ, consider how he was devoted and obedient to God; and how he was full of purity and holiness, unspotted in every way; how he was to his friends and to all who had any goodness in them; and how he prayed for his very enemies.

And as for the devil himself, deal with him as Christ did, that is, have no terms with him, although he comes to us in our nearest friends. He came to Christ in Peter. And Christ said, 'Satan, get behind me' (*Matt.* 16:23). If the devil comes to us in our wives, in our children, in our friends, avoid Satan. He comes to us sometimes in our friends, to give corrupt judgement, to promote selfish causes, to do this or that which may crack our conscience. Let us imitate Christ, and discern between our friends' love and the subtlety of the devil in them, and be able to say, 'Get behind me, Satan.' We see that Christ, when he encountered Satan, fought not with Satan's weapons but with the Word of God. He did not give reproach for reproach, or sophistry for sophistry, but, 'It is written' (*Matt.* 4:4-10), showing that we must counter Satan with God's armoury, with weapons out of the book of God.

And when Satan would confess him, and make much of him, 'Oh, thou art the Son of God,' he would have nothing to do with him. So have nothing to do with those who are manifestly led with the spirit of Satan and would press kindness on us. The devil is not always a liar, but he always defrauds. And those who are led by

[113]

the spirit of the devil do not lie about everything, but there is deceit in everything, for it is all kindness that snares and gifts that harm. All offers from those who are led by the spirit of Satan we ought to suspect. When Christ was offered a kindness by Satan, he said, 'Away, you and your kindness.' So have nothing to do with devilish men. They are always deceivers, though not always liars; and those who see this have least to do with them and are most at ease and prosper most.

So you have a taste of Christ's behaviour to his friends, to his enemies, to Satan. And as for hypocrites he says, 'Woe to them' (*Matt.* 23:13). He hated them above all the proud Pharisees. I might spend much time in going over details in the Gospels, to see what expressions there are of Jesus Christ.

When you read in the Gospels of any expression of his love and gentleness, of his obedience and humility, in washing his disciples' feet, for example, or of his saying 'Learn of me, for I am meek' (*Matt.* 11:29), then think, 'This is the expression of my blessed Saviour, the second Adam, to whose image I must be transformed.' And when you are tempted to sin, from your own corruption or from Satan, reason with yourself: 'Would our blessed Saviour, if he were upon earth, do this? would he say this? would he not be ready to do this good turn? Surely he would; and I must be changed into his image and likeness.' Surely our blessed Saviour would not stain and defile his body. He would not make his tongue an instrument of untruth to deceive others. He would not be covetous and injurious.

Are you a Christian or not? If you are, you have the anointing of Jesus Christ. That anointing that was poured on him as the head, runs down to you as a member, as Aaron's ointment ran down to his skirts. If you are only the skirt of Christ, the lowest Christian, you have the same grace. And you must express Christ; as you partake of his name, so you must partake of his anointing. If you are a Christian, why do you do this? Does it agree with what you profess? Do you carry the image of Satan and think you are a Christian? Are you a Christian in name only? Any true Christian is changed into the likeness of Christ, into his image.

It is good upon all occasions, every day, to think, 'What would my blessed Saviour say if he were here? and what did he do in similar cases when he was upon earth? I must be "led by the Spirit of Christ", or else I am none of his.' Let us be ashamed when we are moved by our corruptions and temptations to do anything contrary to this blessed image.

Consider, the more we grow into the likeness of Christ, the more we grow in the love of God, who delights in us as he does in his own Son: 'This is my beloved Son, in whom I am well pleased' (*Matt.* 3:17). The more we are like Christ, the more he is pleased with us.

And the more we shall grow in love for one another, for the more pictures conform to the original pattern, the more they are like one another. So the more we grow to be like Christ, the more we are like one another; and the more alike, the more love.

Who keeps Christ alive in the world, but a company of Christians, who carry his resemblance? As we say of a child that is like his father, This man cannot die as long as his son is alive, because he resembles his father; so too, as long as Christians are in the world, who have the Spirit of Christ, Christ cannot die. He lives in them, and Christ is alive in the world in no other way than in the hearts of Christians, who have received his grace and who carry the picture and resemblance of Christ in them.

But how are we changed into the likeness of Christ? How do we come to be like him?

When we believe in Christ, we are planted into the likeness of his death and his resurrection. This is somewhat mystical, yet it is taught in the Scriptures, especially in Romans 6. And how do we come to die to sin by virtue of Christ's death and to live to right-eousness by the fellowship of Christ's resurrection? The Scripture says we are transformed into the likeness of Christ. Let us expound these phrases a little.

When Christ died, it was in his own person; Christ died whole and was crucified. But yet the death itself, the crucifying, was limited to the human nature – the human nature died and not the godhead. Yet by reason of the union, whole Christ died and was crucified: the 'Lord of glory' was crucified, as the Scripture says.

And as it was in Christ natural, so it is in Christ mystical. Whole Christ mystical was crucified, and whole Christ mystical is risen again, even though the crucifying was confined to Christ the head, not the members. As his death was limited to his human nature, so this crucifying belonged to the head, and the head rose. Yet all believers – whole Christ – as soon as they are one with Christ by reason of the mystical union, are dead and crucified in Christ their head, and they are risen and sit in heavenly places, in Christ their head.

So a true believer, when he is made one with Christ, reasons: 'My corruption of nature, this natural pride of heart and enmity of goodness, is crucified, for I am one with Christ. I in my head was crucified, and I in my head am now risen and sit in heaven. So now I am in some way glorious and, in my head, I attend to things above. And because the members must conform to the head, I must die to sin more and more, be crucified to sin, and rise by the Spirit of Christ and ascend with him. The more I know and meditate on this, the more I am transformed into the likeness of his death and resurrection.'

Question: What things in Christ's death especially reveal themselves to us, to our comfort, when we believe?

Answer: Three things: wonderful love, that he died for us; wonderful hatred, that he would die for sin; and wonderful holiness and love of grace.

From where does hatred of sin come, but from wondrous purity and holiness that cannot endure sin? And when the soul considers that it is one with Christ, it has the same disposition that Christ had. Christ in love for us died. Can I apprehend that love of Christ when he died and was crucified and tormented for my sin, unless, out of love, I hate sin again? And when I consider how Christ died to purge sin and to satisfy for it, can I, being one with him, have any attitude other than he had upon the cross? I cannot. So, whether I consider his love to me, or the hatred he bore to sin, remembering myself to be one with him by a mystical union, I shall have the same love to him and be like him in every way, to love what he loves, and to hate what he hates.

I cannot but hate sin; and, hating sin, I must re-enact his part. That is, as he died for sin, so I die to sin; as he was crucified for it, so it is crucified in me; as he was pierced, so he gives corruption a stab in me; as he was buried, so my corruption is buried; and as he died once never to die again, so I follow my sins to the grave, to the death of old Adam, that he never rises again. So I say, considering my union with Christ puts Christ's disposition into me and makes me act Christ's part, to die to sin daily more and more. These and similar thoughts are stirred up in a Christian, which St Paul aims at in Romans 6 and other passages.

So by the virtue of Christ's resurrection I am conformed more and more to the graces in him. As the power of God's Spirit raised him up when he was at the lowest, after three days in the grave, so the Spirit in every Christian raises him up at the lowest, to comfort, to a further degree of grace, more and more. When Christians are fallen into any sin or any affliction for sin, when they are tripped and undermined by their corruptions, the same power that raised Christ from the grave raises them from their sins daily, that they gather strength against them. And when we are at the lowest, in the grave, the same power will raise us like Christ in every way. So you see how we are changed to the likeness of Christ.

How shall we know whether we have the image of Christ stamped upon us?

If we are changed into the likeness of Christ, we shall be changed in our understandings, to judge things as he did. His aim was to please his Father in all things. He judged matters of grace and of the kingdom of God above all else, for the soul is of more worth than the whole world. See the judgement that he passed: 'Seek ye first the kingdom of God, and all these things shall be added unto you' (*Matt.* 6:33). If we want to have his image upon us we must be changed in our judgement. We must be like him in our will, in our choice, and in the purpose and resolution of our will. Our souls must be edged and pointed as his was, wholly for heaven and the kingdom of God. And there must be a change in our inclinations; we must love and joy and delight in whatever he did.

The way to stir ourselves up to this is to see what image we naturally carry and to see ourselves in the glass of the law. If a man remembers, 'If Christ's image is not upon me, I carry the image of the devil,' this would make him labour to get another image upon him. For at the day of judgement Christ will not own us if he does not see his image upon us. Caesar will own Caesar's coin if he see his image upon it. ('Whose is this image and superscription? . . . Give unto Caesar that which is Caesar's' [*Matt.* 22:20–21]). If Christ sees his stamp on us, he will own us at the day of judgement, or else not. We are all naturally opposite to Christ, full of pride and malice, of the spirit of the world and the devil. Get this out by all means, or else Christ will not own us at the day of judgement. He will not look on us. He cannot abide to see us if we do not have his image. We must bear the image of the second Adam as we did the image of the first.

The law of God was written on Adam's heart; it is expressed and copied. There we see ourselves. There we see all the curses. There we see ourselves guilty of the breach of every commandment. If we understand the law spiritually, we know that desire of women and vengeful thoughts are murder and adultery. We must understand the law spiritually, and see ourselves in that glass, see ourselves utterly condemned. This will make us fly to the glass of the gospel, that we may be changed into the image of Christ.

There is another image that we desire more to be changed into. We are transformed into the likeness of the world, cast into the mould of the times. We labour to share the current opinions and the ways of advancement of the world. We share the conduct and attitudes of the world, and are moulded to the spirit of the world in all things, so that we might not be observed by others or thwarted in our pleasures and profits. Well, this desire to be transformed into the likeness of the world, to have the spirit of the world, what will it come to in the end?

The world must be condemned. It is the kingdom of Satan, in which he rules. If we want to be damned with the world, let us labour to be transformed into the opinion of the world and to go with the stream and errors of the time. But if we will be saved and have comfort, can we have a better likeness to be transformed into than the image of Christ, by whom we hope to be saved? than to be like him, from whom we hope for so great a matter as salvation?

Use 2. That we may be changed into the likeness of Christ, let us fix our meditations upon him, and we shall find a change, though we do not know how it happens.

As those who are in the sun for work or play find themselves lightened and warmed, so let us set ourselves about holy meditations, and we shall find a secret, imperceptible change; our souls will be altered, we do not know how. There is a virtue that goes with holy meditation, a changing, transforming virtue. And indeed we can think of nothing in Christ without having it change us to the likeness of itself, because we have all from Christ.

Can we think of his humility and not be humble? Can we think, 'Was God humble, and shall base worms be proud? Shall I be fierce when my Saviour was meek?' Can a proud, fierce heart apprehend a sweet, meek Saviour? No. The heart must be suited to the thing apprehended. It is impossible that a heart that is not meek, and sweetened, and brought low, should apprehend a loving and humble Saviour.

There must be a suitability between the heart and Christ. As he was born of a humble virgin, so he is born and conceived in a humble heart. Christ is conceived and born, and lives and grows in every Christian. And a humble and lowly heart made like him by his Spirit, that is the womb. The heart that is suitable is the heart that he is formed in.

Use 3. To be changed into this image, when we are once in the state of grace, let us look to the remainder of our own corruptions.

The best of us shall see things that will make us look after Christ. Look to our worldly-mindedness, to our passions, to our rebellions, to our darkness and deadness of spirit, and then go to Christ. The Lord has appointed Christ to be a head, to be a full vessel, that of his grace we might have grace for grace. He was 'anointed with the oil of gladness above his fellows' (*Psa.* 45:7), but also for his fellows. I am earthly-minded; he is heavenly. I am full of rebellions, of lusts; all is at peace in him. The image of God is perfect in him, and he is a head to infuse grace, a head of influence as well as of eminence. He is not only above me, but he has all grace for me. Therefore, go to Christ. I need thy heavenly-mindedness, and some portion of thy meekness, of thy spiritual strength. I am weak, and dark, and dead, shine on me. Thou hast fullness for me. So draw upon every occasion virtue and life from Christ our head. This is to know what is meant by being transformed to Christ our head.

There are two conformities of exceeding comfort to us, and we must meditate on both.

First, Christ's conformity to us. He was transfigured into our likeness. In love to us he became man, and not only a man, but in the form of a servant. He took man's nature, and man's base condition (*Phil.* 2:8). Here is the ground of our comfort, that Christ took our form, he transfigured himself to our lowliness. Shall not we labour to be transformed, to be like him, who out of love stooped so low as to be like us? Let us but think of this! Our blessed Saviour took our nature on him pure and holy by his Spirit. He followed sin to death. He was conceived, and lived, and died without sin, to satisfy for sin; and now by his Spirit he cleanses out sin. He pursued and chased out sin from his conception through all the passages of his life; so we should be like him. Drive away sin, get the Spirit, that our nature in us may be as it was in him: holy, pure, and spiritual. Shall he be conformed to us, and we not be conformed to him?

Second, there are many reasons and considerations to move us to be changed into the image of Christ. Christ, in this work of changing, is all in all.

First of all, by Christ's death and satisfaction to divine justice, we have the Spirit of God that does all. The Spirit is the gift of God's love and, next to Christ, the greatest. Christ, having reconciled God, God being reconciled, gives the Spirit. Our sins being forgiven, the fruit of God's love is the Spirit. So we have the Spirit by the merit of Christ. Christ receives the Spirit first, and then, as a head, he sends him into our hearts. And from Christ we have the pattern of all grace whatever, to which we are changed.

The reasons inducing us to change are all from Christ. For we are changed not only by power, but by reason. There are the greatest reasons in the world to be a Christian and to come out of the state of nature. When our understanding is enlightened to see the horrible state of nature, and the angry face of God with it, and then to have our eyes opened at the same time to see the glorious and gracious face of God in Jesus Christ, it is the greatest wisdom in the world to come out of that cursed state to a better one. The reasons for this change are from Christ: by knowing Christ, we know the cursed state to be absent from him, and see the glorious benefits by Christ's redemption and glorification. These are set before the eye of the soul, and then the heart stirred by reason says: If Christ gave himself for me, shall not I give myself to Christ? Paul has his heavenly logic, 'Christ died for us, that we might live to him' (*Rom. 6:10–11*). So, in changing to Christ's image, we have the merit of the Spirit from him, the derivation of the Spirit from him as a head, the pattern of grace from him, and the inducing reasons all from Christ.

Since Christ is the image to which we are changed, let us learn, if we would see anything excellent in ourselves, to see it in Christ first. There is nothing excellent in man that is not in Christ first, as the first image, the first receiver of all. If we would see the love of God, see the love of God in Christ our head first, in him that is God's beloved. If we would see the gifts that God has blessed us with, spiritual blessings, it is in Christ. We have it from our head first. God's favour was first in him: 'This is my beloved Son, in whom I am well pleased' (*Matt.* 3:17). I am well pleased in him, and in all his that are one mystical body with him. If we would see our evil done away, our sins removed, see it in Christ abased, in Christ crucified and made a curse. See them all wiped away in the cross of Christ. If we would see glory upon the removal of our sins, see it in Christ first. He is first risen, and therefore we shall rise. He is ascended and sits in heavenly places; therefore we ascend and sit in heavenly places with him.

All that we have or look to have good in us, see it in the first pattern, in Christ. The reason is clear: we are elected and predestined 'to be conformed to the image of his Son' (*Rom.* 8:29), to be conformed to Christ in all things, to be loved as he is, to be gracious as he is. To rise to be glorious, to be freed and justified afterward from all our sins, as he our surety was. We are ordained to be conformed to him every way. In a word, the flesh of Christ was holy; it was a suffering flesh, and now it is a glorious flesh. So our nature must be like this image. It must be flesh sanctified by the same Spirit that sanctified the mass that Christ was made of in the womb. It must be suffering flesh, in conformity to him; for the flesh that he took was suffering flesh, and he had a kingdom of patience before he had a kingdom of glory. So we must go through a kingdom of patience to the kingdom of glory. And then upon conformity in holiness with Christ comes our conformity in glory. When we are content to be conformed to Christ in our suffering flesh, then we shall be conformed to Christ in our glorious flesh; for our flesh must be as his was, holy and patient and suffering, and then it shall be glorious. So in all things we must look to Christ first; he must have the pre-eminence.

Of all contemplations under heaven, there is no contemplation so sweet and powerful as to see God in Christ and Christ first abased for us, and to see ourselves abased in Christ, and crucified in Christ, and acquitted in Christ. And then let us raise our thoughts a little higher, to see ourselves made little by little glorious in Christ; to see ourselves in him rising and ascending and sitting at the right hand of God in heavenly places; to see ourselves, by a spirit of faith, in heaven already with Christ. What a glorious sight and contemplation this is! If we first look upon ourselves as we are, we are as branches cut off from the tree, as a river cut off from the spring, that dies immediately. What is in us, except what we have derived from Christ, who is the first, the spring of all grace, the sum of all the beams that shine upon us? We are as branches cut off. Now to see Christ, and ourselves in Christ, transforms us to be like his image. It is the sweetest contemplation that can be.

And we see that this change is brought about by beholding. Beholding the glory of God in the gospel is a powerful beholding; for, says he, 'we are changed, by beholding', to the image of Christ. Sight works upon the imaginations in brute creatures; as Laban's sheep, when they saw the multi-coloured rods, it worked upon their imaginations, and they had multi-coloured lambs (*Gen.* 30:37–39). Will sight work upon imagination, and imagination work a real change in nature? And shall not the glorious sight of God's mercy and love in Christ work a change in our soul? Is not the eye of faith stronger than natural imagination to alter and change? Certainly the eye of faith, apprehending God's love and mercy in Christ, has a power to change. The gospel itself, together with the Spirit, has a power to change. By it we partake of the divine nature.

This glass of the gospel is excellent and eminent above all other glasses. It is a mirror that changes us. When we see ourselves and our corruptions in the glass of the law, we see ourselves dead. The law finds us dead and leaves us dead; it cannot give us any life. But when we look into the gospel and see the glory of God, the mercy of God, and the gracious promises of the gospel, we are changed into the likeness of Christ, whom we see in the gospel. This excellent glass has a transforming power to make beautiful. Such a glass would be much prized in this proud world; such a glass is the gospel.

So let us love this glass above all other glasses. Nothing can change us but the gospel. The gospel has a changing power, as you see in Isaiah 11: 'the wolf shall live with the lamb' (verse 6) and 'the whole earth shall be full of the knowledge of the Lord' (verse 9). The knowledge of Christ Jesus changes a man even from an intractable, fierce creature, to be tractable, sweet, and companionable.

[125]

It changes us into the likeness of Christ especially in that we see ourselves in the love of Christ and in the love of God. We are moved to be changed not by seeing Christ alone, or by seeing God in Christ alone, but by seeing God's love in Christ to us, and Christ's love to us. The Spirit of faith, given together with the gospel, sees Christ giving himself for me, and sees God the Father's love in Christ, and giving me to Christ. When the Spirit of faith sees God to be mine in Christ, and sees Christ mine, and sees myself in the love of God and of Christ, the soul is stirred up with a holy desire to be like Christ Jesus, who loved me so much, and to be conformed to God all I can. If a person is great and glorious, and is our friend too, we naturally desire to imitate them all we can. And seeing ourselves in the love of God and Christ will naturally stir us up to be like so sweet, and gracious, and loving a Saviour.

Use 4. There are three sights that have a wondrous efficacy. They go together and are the foundation of all comfort:
God sees us in Christ, and therefore loves us as we are in Christ. As God gives us to Christ, he sees us as given to him in his election.

Christ loves us as he sees us in his Father's love. Christ sees us as given of the Father (*John* 17:12) and sees us as his own members.

And we by a Spirit of faith see Christ, and see ourselves in Christ, and see the love of God to us in Christ. And from here comes a desire to imitate and express Jesus Christ. When we look upon the mercy of God in Christ, it kindles love, and love kindles love as fire kindles fire.

The meditation of the glorious love of God in Christ works love, and love effects change; love transforms as fire does. The love of God warms us, and we are fit to have all impressions stamped upon us, like things that are heated. Iron is dull and heavy, yet when hot it is bright and pliable and has as much as possible of the nature of fire upon it. In the same way our dead, dull, inflexible and unyielding souls become malleable and flexible by the love of Christ shining upon them. His love transforms and kindles them.

This is how the glory of God's love in Christ transforms us: the discovery of the abundant mercy in God towards us kindles love to him, and that love works likeness. Love to greatness transforms us because it causes a desire to be like those who are great. Where there is dependence there is a desire to be like, even among men. How much more, then, does it breed a desire to be like Christ in our disposition all we can – considering that God so loves our nature in Christ, and that our nature is so full of grace in Christ, and considering the love of God in Christ, who has done so much for us.

By looking to the glory of God in Christ we see Christ as our husband, and that breeds in us the affections of a spouse. We see Christ as our head, and that breeds a disposition in us to be members like him.

Question: How can we know for certain that we see God in Christ and the glory of God in the gospel?

Answer: Does this sight have a transforming power in you, to make you like the image of Christ? If it does not, it is a barren, empty contemplation that has no efficacy at all. Insofar as the sight of God's love in Christ breeds conformity to Christ, it is gracious and comforting. See whether you are transformed to the image of Christ. If there is no change, there is no beholding of Christ to speak of. No one ever sees the mercy of God in Christ by the eye of faith without being changed.

And as there must be a change, so it must be from beholding the mercy of God in Christ. Can you imagine that any soul can see itself in the glass of God's love in Jesus Christ, can see in the gospel Christ, and in him God reconciled to him in particular, and not love God in return and be altered? It is impossible; such a sight always has an effect. It works love, and love works of imitation. What is it that makes one work to express another in their disposition and conduct? Oh, it is love, as children imitate their parents. Love is full of invention and tries to please the person loved as much as it can in every way. And we desire to be like Christ because we see the glory of God's mercy shining in Christ.

The adversaries of the grace of God quarrel with us, because we preach justification by the free mercy and love of God in Christ. They say this is to deaden the spirits of men, so that they do not care about good works. But can there be any greater incentive and motive in the world to sanctification, to express Christ and to study Christ, than to consider what favour and mercy we have in Christ; how we are justified and freed by the glorious mercy of God in Christ? There cannot be any greater. We see here that they depend upon one another. By seeing in the glass of the gospel the glory of God, we are transformed from glory to glory. An excellent glass the gospel is: by seeing God's love in it we are changed.

The law is a glass too, but the sort of glass that St James speaks of. When one looks into it and sees his duty, he goes away and forgets (*James* 1:23–24). The law reveals our sin and misery. Indeed, it is a true glass; if we look into it we see the true picture of old Adam and of corruption. But this glass does not act upon us. But when the gospel glass is held out by the ministers of the

Word, when people see the love of God in Christ, it changes and transforms them. It makes those who before were deformed and disfigured, who bore the image of Satan, now to be transformed to be like Christ, by whom they must be saved. Is there any study in the world more excellent than that of the gospel and of the mercy of God in Christ, which transform and change people from one degree of grace to another?

As for those who find themselves to be 'old men' still, who have lived, and still live, in corruption, they must not think they have any benefit by the gospel. If they do, they deceive themselves. They never knew God. For whoever says he has communion with God but walks in darkness is a liar, for God is light (*1 John* 1:5–6). How can a man see himself in the love of God and remain in a dark state opposite to love? Will it not alter him? It will not allow him to live in sins against conscience. Let no one who does so think he has benefit by Christ. That knowledge is but a notional knowledge, a speculation. It is not a spiritual knowledge, because wherever the knowledge of God in Christ is real, there is a change and conversion of the whole person. There is a new judgement and new affections. The bent and bias is another way than they were before.

There is a change which in the Scripture is called a turning (*Matt.* 18:3). Those things that were formerly before them are now behind them; and those things that were behind them are now before them. Whereas before, they turned their back upon God and good, now they turn their faces to look toward God and heaven and to a better condition; for this change is nothing else but conversion. Those who have seen Christ, the sight makes them differ from themselves; it works a change.

If there were not a change, it would make God swear

falsely. For according to Zacharias' song, 'He has sworn that, being delivered out of the hands of our enemies, we should serve him without fear, in holiness and right-eousness, all the days of our life' (*Luke* 1:73–75). If anyone says he is delivered from his enemies and thinks he shall not be damned and go to hell, and yet does not live in holiness and righteousness, he makes God's oath useless, for God's oath joins both together: deliverance, and serving without fear – without slavish fear, but with a fear of reverence. All who are in a state of deliverance have grace granted them by which they may serve God in holiness and righteousness all their lives. They are changed into the same image.

'FROM GLORY TO GLORY' (I)

By glory here is meant especially grace, and the accompanying favour of God. When we are persuaded of it by the Spirit, who works grace in us, grace is followed by peace, joy, comfort, and many such things which the Scripture counts glory.

We say there are four degrees of the glory of a Christian.

a) The initial glory is in his *first conversion*, when the Christian knows his deliverance from his cursed and damnable state, and also knows of his title to life everlasting. He comes to have friendship with God. For that, the Spirit must assimilate him to God, in a holy disposition. Now when, upon the favour of God, we come to be friends with God and to have our natures altered and renewed, there follow those glorious qualifications, as peace, joy, consolation in all condi-tions, liberty, and boldness to the throne of grace. This is glory! Is it not a glory to be friends with God and to have God deal with us as friends? to reveal his secrets to us of his love and grace in Christ? to discover the mysteries of his love to us, that were hidden from the beginning of the world? Until our effectual calling, our first conversion, we never know that life-long friendship with God.

And then we have our nature renewed, our shame laid aside. Indeed, sin makes us shameful. It is the dishonour and abasement of the soul. The very change of our nature, to be such as God may delight in, is glory. The image of God is glory. In Romans 3 it is said that since the fall, Adam's sin, we are stripped and deprived of the glory of God, that is, of the image of God, by which we resembled God in holiness. So grace by which we again resemble God, the image and likeness of God, that is the glory of man. If one should ask, What is the best glory of a man, that essential glory that characterises a man indeed? It is the stamp of Christ upon him, the image of the second Adam in his soul, to be like him.

And then those glorious qualifications follow: glorious peace, and glorious joy; glorious and unspeakable comfort triumphing and prevailing above all discomforts whatever that we meet with in this world. What can be set against the wrath of God, against hell and damnation, but the comforts of the gospel? Now when a man is in the state of grace and these glorious things follow him, sweet and glorious peace that passes understanding, that all the world and all the devils in hell cannot shake, and joy in the Holy Ghost, and comforts above all discomforts whatever; and when he has glorious liberty to come into the presence of God upon all occasions, being a friend of God – are not these things glorious? And they belong to every Christian.

b) There is a further degree of glory as a Christian *grows in assurance* of his salvation and further friendship with God, and further peace and joy and comfort. The growth of grace is glory. In 2 Peter 1, he follows the point. When we add grace to grace, he says it gives a further entrance into the kingdom of God. For the kingdom of God is begun in grace here, and the further we grow in grace, the more we enter into the kingdom of grace; and the further we enter into that, the nearer we are to the kingdom of glory.

c) The next degree of glory is when the soul enjoys *the presence of God in heaven*.

d) Then the upshot and consummation of all is at *the day of judgement*, when body and soul shall be united again. Then is perfect glory. Here it is insinuated, when he says we are changed from glory to glory, that is, from grace to grace, till all ends in glory, which is the perfection of all in heaven, when body and soul shall both be glorious; 'from glory to glory'.

In this it is considered, first, that grace is glory; and then that grace, being glory, is growing in a continual course till it comes to perfection. We grow 'from glory to glory', from one degree of grace to another.

Grace by which we resemble Christ is glory; indeed it is, for the image and likeness of God is our glory. What was Adam's glory but his likeness to God? He was created in God's image. And what is our glory? To be like Christ. Therefore grace is our glory.

Man's perfection is his glory. But man's perfection is the renewing of God's image in grace. That is why it is his glory.

That which makes a man terrifying to all opponents whatever is glory. Grace makes a man terrible [i.e. terrifying] to the devil and to wicked men, both grace in a man, and grace in the church; for the church is 'terrible, like an army with banners' (*Song of Sol.* 6:4). When the ordinances of God are set up in glory and there is glorious obedience to them in the church, it is terrifying to the enemies as an army with banners; for there is a lustre and glory in all that is God's, both in the believers themselves and likewise in the ordinances of God.

Grace is glorious. As the wise man says, 'Wisdom makes a man's face to shine' (*Eccles.* 8:1). Is not wisdom a glorious thing: a wise, understanding man able to guide himself and others? It puts a beauty upon a man, to be wise and understanding. Humility makes a man glorious, for it makes God put glory upon a man, and a man is glorious and does not realise it. Moses, when his face shined, did not know himself that it shined. Many humble men are glorious and do not think so; they are glorious and they shine, though they do not see it.

Is it not a glorious thing to be taken out of ourselves, to deny ourselves, to offer a holy violence to ourselves and to our corruptions? Is it not glorious, when others lie grovelling like slaves under their corruptions, to stand unmoveable in all the changes of the world and in all kinds of trouble, to stand as a rock in the midst of all, founded upon the love of God in Christ and the hope of glory after? Not to be shaken with the wind of temptations from his standing, at least not to be shaken off his standing – this is glorious, to have a constant spirit.

Is it not glorious to have admittance boldly by grace, to go into the presence of God at all times, to prevail with God? Faith overcomes not only the world but God himself. It binds him with his own promise. Is not faith a glorious grace, that triumphs over the great God himself, binding him with his own Word and promise?

Is not love a glorious grace, that melts one into the likeness of Christ? It constrains, it has a kind of holy violence in it. We shall glory in sufferings for what we

[133]

love. No water, nothing can quench that holy fire that is kindled from heaven. It is a glorious grace.

Hope, what does it do? When it casts anchor in heaven, it keeps us in all the waves. It purges our natures to be like the thing hoped for.

There is no grace that is not glorious. So grace is glory. The image of God is glory. It makes a man glorious. It makes him shine.

Think of one like Joseph, of a sweet, wise, and loving spirit. It is an excellent state to see a man in his place in the commonwealth. What a glorious sight is it to see a Joseph, a Nehemiah, to see a man like Paul, all on fire for the glory of God and the good of the church! The care of all the churches lay upon him. The thought of a man shining in grace, what a glorious thought it is!

And the same is true in men now living. When wisdom and love tend to the common good, when there is a spirit of mortification, when a spirit of love is not for itself but all for the good of others, above self-love, as in Christ, who 'went about doing good' (*Acts* 10:38), it makes them lovely and glorious. Nothing in the world is so glorious as a man in whom the image of Christ is; it puts a glory upon him.

Besides that, it puts an inward glory upon a man, when it makes him rejoice: 'The Spirit of glory rests upon him' (*Isa.* 61:1). Indeed, in imprisonments and abasements, a good man in any condition is glorious. His conduct is glorious. You shall not see flesh and blood, no vengeful mood. When flesh and blood is subdued and nothing appears in a man but the image of Christ, he is a glorious creature, even in the greatest abasement that can be. When Paul was in the stocks, what a glorious condition he was in, when he sung at midnight when the Spirit of glory was upon him!

To see the martyrs suffer without revenge, pray for

their enemies, show a triumphant spirit that conquered all wrongs, and fear of death, and displeasure of men; a spirit above all things below, raising them above encouragements and discouragements – what a glorious thing this was! A man in his right principles, with the image of God upon him, sees all things here below as beneath him. This is glorious, to see a man who overcomes the world, who cares no more for the offers of advancement on the one hand or for threatenings on the other. All this is nothing to him. He breaks it as Samson did his cords. Is this not glorious, to see such a victorious and glorious spirit, above all earthly things whatsoever, that tramples the world under foot, as the 'woman clothed with the sun' treads the 'moon under her feet' (*Rev.* 12:1)?

The church clothed with Christ, who is the glory of the church, tramples all earthly things under foot. Grace is victorious and conquering, prevailing over those corruptions that prevail over ordinary men. A Christian like David, when he had Saul in the cave, overcomes himself (*1 Sam.* 24:4). It shows a great strength of grace. Christ overcame himself on the cross. He prayed for his enemies. So when the nature of man is so subject to the power of grace that though there are rebellions in us – and there will be while we are in this world – still they cannot overpower the principle of grace. All this while a man is a glorious Christian, because he is not subject to the common infirmities and weaknesses of men. It makes a Christian glorious when he brings every thought and affection, and every corruption that may be, to the subjection of the Spirit of glory, to the Spirit of Christ in him. Though old Adam stirs in him, he brings him down, so that he does not scandalise the gospel and what is professed, or weaken the love of good things in the hearts of others. It shall not break out; he subjects these rising thoughts. Here grace is glorious.

Another person cannot do this. He cannot love God; he cannot deny himself; he cannot resist temptations, not inwardly. He may refrain from an action out of fear, but a Christian can love, and fear, and delight in good things. And he can resist, and he can enjoy the things of this life, remembering that they are subordinate to better things. A person outside of grace cannot do that. There is a glory upon a Christian, a derivative glory from Christ. For we shine in his beams. We are changed according to his image 'from glory to glory'.

Objection: It is not doubted that grace is glorious, but it may be objected, Does grace make one glorious? Then why does the world despise those who have grace, those who are like Christ?

Answers:

a) I answer, that it is *from blindness*, from spiritual drunkenness and madness. They cannot discern things; they are besotted; they see no difference. That is why they cannot discern things that are excellent. But take a man in his right principles, take a sober man, and he will see an excellency in a Christian above himself.

b) Grace is often not made so much of in the world because *it is joined with so many infirmities*. Our life 'is hid with Christ' (*Col.* 3:3). It is often hidden under infirmities and under afflictions and does not appear so much in this world.

c) However men force upon themselves a contempt of grace and of the best things, yet notwithstanding *it is indeed forced*; for their conscience stoops at it. Witness conscience when it gives evidence on their deathbed. Take a man when he is himself, when he is sober, when he is best able to judge, when those things are taken

from him that obscured and darkened his judgement –
then he will justify all things that are good, both grace
and the means of grace.

d) It must be so, that the world despises those who
have grace, *that we may be conformed to Christ.* The world
misjudges the state of Christians, thinking them vile and
low. So they did Christ, the head of the church. You see
what they thought of him. His glory was veiled with our
nature and with misery a while, but it sparkled out often
in his miracles. Now this was so that he might suffer and
perform the work of salvation; for the devil or the
wicked world would never have done what they did to
him if his glory had broken forth in its full lustre.

So it is with the mystical body of Christ. The world
misjudges them. It does not appear now what they shall
be hereafter, or what they are now indeed; because
God wants them conformed to Christ. If the glory of
Christians were revealed in true lustre, who would
wrong a Christian? If they saw him indeed to be a
member of Christ and an heir of heaven, the concern of
angels and the price of Christ's death; if they saw
him in his excellency, all the world would admire him
and make even more of him than of potentates and
monarchs! But then, how would he be conformed to his
head in afflictions? The head was to save us by death. He
must be abased. The world must take him as a stranger,
and we that must be conformed to him must pass
as unknown men in the world. But not always so unknown; grace breaks out sometimes and is admired and
imitated. And when it is not imitated, it stirs up envy
and malice in others, the children of the devil.

So, despite all objections, grace is glory. It makes us
like Christ, who is glorious, who is 'the Lord of glory'.

And then it draws glory with it, glorious peace,
comfort and joy in the Holy Ghost, the effects of grace

in the hearts of God's people. As I said, is it not a glorious thing for a man to have that peace in him that passes all understanding, that will settle and quiet his soul when everything is turned upside down? For a Christian to stand unmoveably built upon the rock – where does this ability come from, but from grace? Grace and peace: one follows the other. To have inward joy and comfort in the midst of afflictions and disconsolation is wonderful and glorious. It is called 'joy unspeakable'(*1 Pet.* 1:8). In regard of what follows it, then, in this world grace is glory.

That is why the wise man says that 'the righteous is more excellent than his neighbour'. He is more glorious than another man, as pearls are above pebbles. He is glorious in life; more glorious in death, when his soul shall be put into glory in heaven; and most of all glorious when Christ shall come to be glorious in his saints (*2 Thess.* 1:10).

Another man, who is only a man, carries the image either of a beast or of the devil, besides that of a man. A righteous man that has the image of God stamped upon him is better than another man in every way, for he is in a higher rank of creatures. Grace sets a man as far above other men as other men are above other creatures. At first the creatures revered God in Adam. They came and took their names from him and were subject to him. Grace is a glorious, majestic thing. Wicked men, even Herod, revered grace in John the Baptist (*Mark* 6:20), and evil men revere it in their hearts in God's people, though their mouths speak against it. A Christian is a spiritual man. As reason lifts a man above other creatures, so the image of God set upon a man lifts and raises him above other men.

USES

*Use 1. If grace and the image of God and Christ in us are
glory and make us excellent, let us all labour for grace above
all things.*

We all, as I said before, desire liberty; and as we desire
liberty, so we desire glory; but we do not know how to
come to them. In seeking liberty, we seek licence; in
seeking glory, we seek it from men who cannot give it,
from outward things that are nothing. What is the glory
of all outward things, but the shining of a rotten piece of
wood in the night time, or as a glow-worm? What is all
this glory but a flash? It is nothing. But to seek true glory
indeed, as naturally all do, let us seek grace. It is by grace
that we resemble Christ, the Lord of glory; by grace we
are glorious in the eyes of Christ; by grace we are
glorious both without and within. Though this glory for
the present is hidden, by grace we are terrifying to the
devil and all enemies. Ever since his head was crushed by
Christ, who broke the serpent's head, he is afraid of
man's nature in Christ. He is afraid of Christians,
knowing that they are better than himself. And he shall
be judged by them before long; the devil shall be judged
by Christians. So then, let us strive for this glory. A man
is never glorious till he is a Christian.

It is said that Antiochus was a vile person. What,
though he was a king? Yes. A man may be ever so great
in the world, but if he is a wicked man, a man who
dishonours his tongue, which should be his glory, and
who dishonours and defiles his body, which should be
the temple of the Holy Ghost (*1 Cor.* 6:19); and if he
carries a malicious and malignant spirit and has the
image of the devil in his soul; then however great a
person he is, he will be vile before long, when all shall
end in death. All excellencies must be laid down in

death. Seeing that all other excellencies cannot keep a person from being vile, let us labour for that which will put a glory upon us, for the image of Christ to be stamped upon our soul. There is a great trend in this age in looking to pieces of workmanship. If a man has skill to discern a work of art, it is more than ordinary. What a vanity this is. And what is this compared to having the glorious image of Christ stamped upon us, to be glorious in the eye of God and in the very judgement of carnal men!

Use 2. Oppose this to the scorn and hatred of the world – base-minded persons disgrace and slander goodness so that their own corruption is not so obvious.

Set the judgements of God's Spirit that counts grace glory against all the judgement of the base world. One day they shall know that those whom they now despise shall judge them, and their hearts secretly tell them so. What makes them malign people better than themselves? They have a secret thought, he is above me. 'The spiritual man judges all things' (*I Cor.* 2:15). He discerns with a spiritual eye. He judges and condemns my ways, and hereafter he will judge me. A secret conscience in him makes him fear a good man. Though he demeans and maligns him, his heart stoops.

Use 3. It teaches us how to regard ourselves.

Is grace glory? When God sets it on us, shall we cast our crown in the dirt? Shall we defile and blemish our glory by sinning against conscience? We forget our excellency, that grace is glory. If there is grace in us, we should be honourable to ourselves; that is, Christians should remember their holy state. What! I that am an heir of heaven; I that am a king; I that am a conqueror; I that am a son of God; I that am a freeman: should I tangle myself with these things? Shall I go and stain myself? Is it not unsightly to see a golden pillar daubed with dirt, or a crown cast into the dirt? God has put a crown upon me; he has made me a king; he has made me an heir of heaven; he has made me his son; he has put a glory upon me. Shall I abase myself in low devilish courses? No. I will be more honourable in my own eyes. Let us think ourselves too good for the base service of Satan. We should take these thoughts. They are not proud, but befitting our condition. When we are tempted to any low course, whatever it is, it is contrary to our calling.

Use 4. Let us comfort ourselves in the work of grace, though it is in ever so poor a measure, and so disparaged by the world. Those who are besotted with false vainglory have the eyes of their souls dazzled and blinded by it. They cannot judge the glory of a Christian; they lack the sight for it. So let us be content to pass in the world as hidden. Christ passed concealed in the world; only now and then did the beams of his glory break forth in his miracles. So we must be content. Our glory is hidden in Christ for the most part, and it is clouded with the reproach and malice of men and sometimes with infirmities, as it will be in this world. Let us comfort ourselves that we are glorious nonetheless, and glorious within; and this glory will break out in a holy manner of life. And it is better to be glorious in the eyes of God and angels and good men, and in the consciences of ill men, than to have glory from their mouths.

Malice will not allow them to glorify them with their mouths, but their consciences must bow to goodness, for God has put a majesty into goodness. Any man who is a man and not a beast, and has natural principles, will reverence it, and the consciences of such men will make them speak the truth one day. They shall say, 'We fools thought these men mad, but now we see ourselves fools.'

So in the disparagements of worldly men, who do not know where true glory lies, let us comfort ourselves and be content with this, that God has made us truly glorious by working a change in some measure.

Use 5. We may know whether or not we have grace in us.
The Spirit of God and the truth of God change our nature so that we count grace glory. This very judgement shows that there is an alteration in our affections, that we are changed in the spirit of our minds and have a right notion of heavenly things. No one but a Christian indeed can judge grace to be glory. If a man truly thinks grace to be glory, if he is convinced by the power of the Spirit, he has grace. For there is an instinct in all men to glory in something. The fools of the world glory in something, in beastly courses. Some devilish men glory that they can circumvent others. Rather than have no glory, men will glory in that which is shame indeed. Man having a disposition always to glory in something, if he is convinced that grace is glory, he will be gracious.

Examine your own souls and see what conceptions you have of the image of God and the graces of Christianity, and then certainly it will raise a holy ambition to have that stamp set upon you.

Another evidence that a man has grace is that he can look upon the life of another who is better than he, and see it and love it as glory. Many men see grace in others, but with a maligning eye. They see it to disgrace it. For naturally this is in men. They are so vainglorious and ambitious that when they see the lives of others outshine theirs, instead of imitating, they obscure and darken that light with slander. This is in the prouder and greater sort of men. What grace they will not imitate,

they will defame. They will not be outshined by anything. Men can endure good things in books and by
reports, and good things of men that are dead, but they
cannot endure good things right in front of their eyes.
Especially when it comes to competition and comparison, they love to outshine others.

But for those who can see so far into the life of
another man as to love it and honour the grace of God
there, it is a sign that some work of glory is begun in
them.

'FROM GLORY TO GLORY' (2)

We see that the state of God's children both here and in
heaven is called glory. The children of God are kings
here, they shall be kings in heaven. They are saints here,
as they are saints in heaven. There is an adoption of
grace as well as an adoption of glory (*Rom.* 8). There is a
regeneration now of our souls; there is a regeneration
then of soul and body. We are new creatures here; and
we shall be new creatures there.

Question. Why do both come under one name, the
state of glory in heaven and the state of grace here? Is
there no difference?

Answer. Yes, but the difference is only in degree, for
heaven must be begun here. If we mean ever to enter
into heaven hereafter, we enter into the suburbs here.
We must be new creatures here. We are kings here;
we are heirs apparent here; we are adopted here; we
are regenerate here; we are glorious here, before we are
glorious hereafter. We may read our future state in our
present. We must not think to come out of the filth of sin
to heaven, but heaven must be begun here.

Would you like to know what your condition shall be
afterwards? Read it in your present disposition. If there

is not a change, and a glorious change, here, never look for a glorious change hereafter. What is not begun in grace shall never be accomplished in glory. Both grace here and glory hereafter come under the same name.

And also it is a reason for comfort: Why do we have the same term here? When we are in the state of grace, why are we adorned with the same title as we shall be in heaven? It is partly for certainty. Grace is glory, and its perfection is glory, to show that where grace is truly begun it will end in glory. All the powers in the world cannot interrupt God's gracious progress. What is begun in grace will end in glory. Where the foundation is laid, God will be sure to put up the roof. He never repents of his beginnings. Solomon said that the righteous is like the sun that grows brighter and brighter till it comes to its full strength (*Prov.* 4:18). So the state of the godly grows more and more, from light to light, till he comes to full strength.

The state of the wicked is completely contrary. The state of the wicked is like the declining day. The sun goes down and down to twilight, and then to darkness, and then to utter darkness. So, being dark in themselves, they grow from the darkness of misery and terror of conscience to eternal, black, dismal darkness in hell.

But the state of the godly is like the course of the sun after midnight, which is going up and up still, till it comes to midday. So the state of the godly is always a growing state; it is a hopeful condition. They go from glory to glory. So let us be assured of eternal glory for the time to come, as we are sure of the beginnings of grace here.

You see, then, the main difference between the godly and others. Others grow backward, from worse to worse, till they end in utter desolation and destruction for ever. But the godly rise by degrees till they come to that happiness that can admit no further degrees. All the glory of the world ends in vanity and nothing. But the glory of a Christian that begins in grace proceeds from glory to glory, always growing and improving. If men were not spiritually mad, would they not rather be in a condition always growing more and more hopeful still, than to be in a condition always declining, and most subject to decline when it is at the top? God's children are near rising when they are at the lowest. A spirit of glory lights and rests on them. It does not light upon them and then go away. It is not as a flash or a blaze of flax. But the Spirit rests and grows still upon them 'from glory to glory'. The state of a Christian soundly converted is comforted when he thinks, 'Every day brings me nearer my glory; every day I rise I am somewhat happier than I was the day before, because I am somewhat more glorious and nearer to eternal glory'; whereas a wretch that lives in sins against conscience may say, 'I am somewhat nearer hell, nearer eclipsing, and ebbing, and declining than before.' So every day brings comfort to the one, and terror to the other.

Grace, we see, is glory, and the more grace grows, and the more it shines, the more glory.

We say of fire, the more it burns the less it smokes. The less infirmity appears that may disgrace it, the more grace; and the more light and lustre, the less infirmity. Glory belongs to the growth of grace in this world. Is not a Christian a glorious Christian when he is a grown Christian; when he gives out a lustre as a pearl; when as a glorious light he shines to the example of others; and when he is able to say, as Paul says gloriously of himself, 'I can do all through Christ which strengtheneth me' (*Phil.* 4:13), to want and to abound? Cast him into any condition you will, he is like himself. Cast Joseph into prison, he is Joseph still. Cast Paul in the dungeon, he is Paul still and is never more glorious than in the midst of afflictions. So grace growing to some perfection is glorious. 'Wisdom maketh a man's face to shine,' says Solomon (*Eccles.* 8:1). So it is true of all other graces in some perfection. They make a man shine.

There is nothing in the world so glorious as a Christian who is grown to some perfection. Indeed, he is so glorious that the eye of the world, when looking upon him, is stirred to envy. When carnal persons see a Christian unmoveable in the midst of all motions, and unchangeable in all changes, when nothing can alter him, but he goes on, they are in wonder at the condition of this man, whose grounds and resolutions are indeed above all the world's discouragements and encouragements.

David was a king and a prophet; he was a holy man, and he was ruddy and handsome. David was a king of a great people and was excellent in many ways. Oh, but what does David account the prerogative of a man? Blessed is the man whose sins are forgiven, in whose spirit there is no guile (*Psa.* 32: 1,2) – that is, the man who is truly sanctified in spirit, who is justified, and as a witness of the forgiveness of his sins, has a spirit without guile. Happy is that man, not who is a king or a prophet, or a strong or handsome man, or has this or that endowment– but happy is the man whose sins are forgiven and whose spirit is sanctified.

We see then that there must be an increase, a growing 'from glory to glory'. There is no stop or standstill in religion. There must of necessity be a desire to grow better and better; for glory will grow still to glory. Grace will never cease till it ends in glory.

In our own dispositions, we desire it to increase more and more the image of God and Christ in us.

[146]

And grace ends in glory according to God's purpose. Where he begins he makes an end. We look to him who will not have us in a state of imperfection. He has called and chosen us not to imperfection, but to perfection. He has elected us to perfection. He has chosen us to be spotless, not to be conflicting with our corruptions, to be always halting like Jacob. We shall have perfect strength. So there is no standing still in religion; there must be a perpetual growth.

And we desire it and strive for it . It is inbred in all things that are imperfect to move to perfection till they come to their full maturity. We see it in grain, weak grain. Till it comes to its full growth, it breaks through clods, through things harder than itself. Corn and seeds have a beginning of life of their own kind in them. Till those seeds come to growth, they put out themselves with a great deal of strength against opposition. Grace, too, is of such a strong nature. Intended by God for perfection, it will not rest in low beginnings but puts itself forward and breaks through opposition. You see the necessity of it. There must be a growth from glory to glory.

At the first regeneration, when we first have grace, there is the beginning of a new life and there are seeds of all graces. But this growth is especially in intensity and extension. Grace grows more and more in strength, and it extends itself further and further to the use of many. I say, grace grows in its depth and strength and reaches itself to the use of more. The more a Christian lives, when he is in a right state and disposition as a Christian should be, he is stronger in all particular graces, and does the more good and shines more in his life to others.

And, as there is growth in intensity and extension, so there is growth in the quality and purity of grace. The longer a man lives, those graces that he has grow more refined. When a Christian is a new Christian, he has the taste of the old stock. The fruit of righteousness that comes from a man at his first conversion tastes a great deal of old Adam. It savours of the old stock. But the more he lives and grows spiritual, the more what comes from him relishes of the Spirit, the more refined is his wisdom, the more refined is his love, joy and delight.

Objection. Here we may answer the objection that an old man seems not to grow in grace. He seems not to be so good a man, not as zealous as when he was young.

Answer. In those who are young there is a great deal of nature joined with a little grace, and that grace in them is expressed more noticeably because it is carried with the current of nature. But in age, in grown Christians, it is more refined. The knowledge they have is more pure and more settled, and their love and affection is more refined. There is less self-love, and the zeal they have is joined with more heavenly discretion. There is less wild fire, less strange fire with it. Though there is less heat of nature, so that it is not so outwardly demonstrated to the eye of the world, it is more refined and pure. So grace grows in purity and perfection, though it is not altogether pure; something savouring of the worst principle in nature will stick to our best performances. We carry flesh and spirit always, so that what comes from us will savour of corruption; yet this is less so in a grown Christian, a father in Christianity, than in another.

Grace is glory with regard to the state before. The least degree of grace is glory with regard to the state of nature. But grace is not glory properly until it grows.

With regard to the state of nature, grace is glory even at its lowest. For is it not a glory for a man to be taken into the fellowship of Christ? to be a son of God and an heir of heaven? to have angels for his attendants? to be begotten by the glorious gospel, the Word of God, that immortal seed? Is he not glorious who has God the Father, and God the Son, the Lord of glory, and the Holy Ghost, the Spirit of glory, and the glorious gospel, and glorious angels for his attendants? Every Christian has all these. So grace is a kind of glory.

Yet we must not content ourselves with that. Grace is then especially glory when it comes to growth. We must labour that grace may appear. What is glory? Properly, glory is excellency and victory manifested. A man is said to be glorious in grace when his grace comes to be noticeably excellent and victorious.

USES

Use 1. Though grace is glory in respect to the former state, still within the rank of Christians we ought to labour to be glorious, that is, to have more and more grace.
We should be more gracious that God may have the more glory from us; and the more grace, the more esteem from him, because we resemble him. And the more glorious we are, the more we resemble Christ Jesus.

Let us labour to be more glorious, also with regard to the church, whom we shall benefit more. The more we grow in grace, the more we shall prevail with God by our prayers. Who prevailed more with their prayers than such men as Moses? And when grace is glorious, that is, when victory is fully manifested, the more we are fit to give a lustre and light, so that others seeing it may glorify God; and the more we may draw others to the love of grace, when they see grace glorious. Grace is then glorious in us that others may be encouraged. It is a glorious thing when we can resist strong temptations, when we are not like children 'carried away with every wind of doctrine' (*Eph.* 4:14). Grace is glorious when a Christian can hold his own in the worst times, when it is a wise thing to be a Christian. As Hilary said in a time of schism, 'it required a great deal of wit [wisdom] to be a Christian', it requires a great deal of wit and study to hold a man on in Christianity.

Though grace is glory, that must not content us, but we must labour to have such a measure of glory as to be glorious in our own rank. Is it not a glorious thing when a man can break through doubts and fears that so trouble other folk? The sun is said to be in glory when it is high; there are many clouds in the morning, but when the sun is at its height at noonday, it scatters them all. So a Christian is in his glory and exaltation when he can scatter doubts, fears and terrors that trouble other weak beginning Christians. When we are troubled with scruples, with this and that, we should labour to get out of them, so that grace may be glorious, to show that we have such a light and convincing knowledge, and that we are so rooted in faith and grace that the Spirit of Christ in us has broken through all these clouds and mists and made us glorious.

Our glory is not like a torrent that runs at full force for a time and then is dried up for ever. Grace continues and increases. As the stream with which it is fed is an ever-living spring, so is grace. It is fed with the grace in Christ; and he is a never-dying spring, a fountain, for that grace in him is fed with his divinity. Where Christ has opened a spring in the heart, he will feed that grace perpetually.

Use 2. Let no one in whom grace has begun be discouraged. God will go on with his own grace. When he has begun a good work, he will finish it to the day of the Lord (*Phil.* 1:6). Though grace is little at first, it shall not stay there.

How it grows we do not know, but at last it is glorious indeed. Until grace has grown it is little distinguished from other things, just as there is little difference between weeds and herbs before they have grown. Grace is little at first, as a grain of mustard seed (*Matt.* 13:31). Jerusalem is not built in a day, as we say of Rome.

Some Christians of a weaker sort want to be in Canaan just as soon as they are out of Egypt, and I cannot blame them. But they are dissatisfied. As soon as they have grace in them they want, out of spiritual covetousness, to advance immediately. 'Oh', they say, 'that I had more knowledge and more victory!' These desires are good; for God does not put desires into the hearts of his children in vain. But they must be content to be led from glory to glory, from one degree of grace to another. Christ himself grew more in favour with God and man. As that little stone grew to a mountain (*Dan.* 2:35), so we must be content to grow from grace to grace. Progress is gradual in the new creature. We cannot immediately be in Canaan. God will lead us through the wilderness, through temptations and crosses, before we come to heaven. Many who see themselves far short of other, stronger Christians think they have no grace at all.

So, though they are short of many that are before them, let those who are growing not be discouraged with their over-little beginnings. It is God's way in this world to bring his children by little and little, through many stations. As they were led in the wilderness from place to place, so God brings his children by many places to heaven. It is one part of a Christian's meekness to be subject to God's wisdom in this respect, and not to complain that they are not as perfect as they would like to be or as they shall be. Rather they should magnify the mercy of God that there is any change in such defiled and polluted souls; that he has granted any spiritual light of understanding, any love of good things; that the bent of their affections is contrary to what it was; that God has granted any beginnings. Magnify his mercy, rather than quarrel with his dispensation, that he does not do all this at once. And, indeed, if we enter into our own hearts, we find it is our fault that we are not more perfect. But let us labour to be meek, and say, 'Lord, since thou hast ordained that I shall grow from glory to glory, from one degree of grace to another, let me have grace to magnify thy mercy that thou hast given me any goodness, rather than to complain that I have no more.' And let us be content in the use of means and make efforts to grow further, though we do not have as much as others have. No, we may not be discouraged, because of the weakness of grace

Nor may we be discouraged with a seeming interruption in our spiritual growth. God sometimes works by contraries. He makes men grow by their decreasing, and to stand by their falls. Sometimes when God will have a man grow he will allow him to fall, that by his fall he may grow in a deeper hatred of sin and in jealousy over his own heart, and in a nearer watchfulness over his own ways; that he may grow more in love with God for pardoning him, and stronger in his resolution; and that he may grow more in humility. No one grows so much as those who have their growth stopped for a time.

Let no one who is stopped be discouraged, but consider that God is working grace of another kind. The Spirit appears and grows in one grace but not in another. As the juice of the herbs runs to the root in the winter, to the leaves in the spring, and to the seed in the autumn, as the life in the plant sometimes appears in one part and sometimes in another, so the Spirit of God appears sometimes in humility, sometimes in joy, sometimes in spiritual strength and courage. Let no one be too discouraged who finds a stop. There is no interruption altogether of the Spirit, and this little interruption is like a sickness that will make them grow and shoot up more afterwards. It draws out the toxins that hinder growth. There is such a mystery in the carrying of men from glory to glory, that it makes them more glorious sometimes by base sins. So I would not have anyone discouraged. Indeed, God will work so that he will wish he had not given him occasion to show his strength in his weakness, his glory in his shame. But God will go through with the work he has begun and will turn everything to good.

And to encourage us here, grace begun has the same name as grace perfected. Both are glory. Why does God call them by one name? To encourage Christians. He tells them that if it is begun it is glory; not that it is already so, but if it is begun it shall never end till it comes to heaven. God calls grace, from the highest to the very beginnings, by the same name, to encourage Christians. If they are within the door of the temple, though they are not as far as those in high and glorious places, still they are going there. Christians can know that unavoidably and indefeasibly they shall come to perfection of glory if it is begun. God looks on Christians not as they are in their imperfections and beginnings, but as that which in time he means them to be. He intends to bring them to glory. That is why he gives grace the name of glory. In the creatures God did not look on the seeds as such, but he looked on them as seeds that he meant to make trees of. And when God looks upon his children, he looks on them not as children, but as they shall be, having come to the perfect stature of Christ. He views us at once in our beginnings and perfections. It is all presented to him at once. So he gives one name to the whole state of grace, grace and glory; all is glory. If there is any goodness, then, any blessed change in us, let us be comforted, for he who has brought us to the beginnings of glory will never fail till he has brought us to perfect glory in heaven, and there our change shall rest. There is no further change there, when we are in our element.

Even as God, when he made man, rested from all his work upon the Sabbath, man being his excellent piece; so the Spirit of God will rest from sanctifying and altering us. Once we are in heaven, in that eternal Sabbath, then we shall need no changes from glory to glory. We shall for ever be filled with the fullness of God.

Until that time, there is no creature in the world so changeable as a Christian. For, first, you see he was made in God's image and likeness in his state of standing. After he fell, there was a change to his second state, that of sin. After the fall, there is a change to the state of grace; and after that from one degree of grace to another in this world till he dies. And then the soul is more perfect and glorious. But at the last, when body and soul shall be united, there shall be an end of all alteration.

So we see that God intends by his Spirit to bring us, though little by little, to perfection of glory as far as our nature is capable, and this shall be at the latter day.

Question: Why not before? Why not in this world?

Answer: We are not capable here of that fullness of glory. St Peter on the mount had only a glimpse of the glory of heaven, and he was spiritually drunk as it were; he did not know what he was saying (*Mark* 9:6). We are not capable. We must grow here from glory to glory till we come to that perfection of glory. God, who gives us the pledge and earnest, could complete the bargain here if we were capable of it, but we are not. God wills to have a difference between the militant church and the triumphant church, and will train us up here to live the life of faith, till we come to live the life of sight, the life of vision for ever in heaven.

Since God by his Spirit is changing us to the likeness of Christ, till he brings us to perfection of glory in heaven, oh, let us comfort ourselves in our imperfections here. We are here lame Mephibosheths. He was a king's son, but he was lame. We are spiritually lame and defective, though we are a king's sons. But what a comfort is this in our imperfections, that as every day we live in this world cuts off a day of our life, so every day we live brings us nearer to heaven. Is this not a sweet comfort? Let us comfort ourselves with these things.

Use 3. If the state of God's people is so sweet and comfortable, and full of well-grounded hopes that glory shall go further on to glory and end in glory, then why should we be afraid of death? For grace will end in glory.

A low glorious estate will be swallowed up in a truly glorious estate. Indeed, grace is swallowed up by glory even as rivers are swallowed up by the ocean. Glory takes away nothing, but perfects everything by death. Why should we be afraid of death? We are afraid of our glory, and of the perfection of our glory.

There are degrees of glory. There is glory begun here in grace, and there is the glory of the soul after death, and the glory of both soul and body for ever in heaven, and each of these makes way to the next. A Christian is glorious while he lives, and he grows in glory while he lives. He is more glorious when he dies, for then his soul has the image of Christ perfectly stamped upon it. But he is most glorious at the day of resurrection, when body and soul shall be glorious, when he shall outshine the very sun itself. All glory shall be nothing to the glory of the saints. They 'shall shine as the sun in the firmament' (*Dan.* 12:3). And indeed there will be no glory but the glory of Christ and of his bride. All other glory shall vanish and come to nothing. But when the spiritual marriage shall be accomplished, the king of heaven and his queen whom he has chosen to himself eternally shall be for ever glorious together.

Why then should we be afraid of death? For then there will be a further degree of glory of the soul, and after that a further degree of body and soul, when our bodies shall be conformed to the glorious body of Christ, when they shall be spiritual (*1 Cor.* 15:44). Let us learn this, to comfort ourselves against those dark times of death, when we shall see an end of all other glory. All worldly glory shall end in the dust and lie down in the grave; we must say that corruption is our father and the worm is our mother (*Job* 17:14). We can claim no other kin with regard to our body; but then with regard to our souls we shall be more glorious. Christ shall put a robe of glory upon us, and then afterward we shall be more glorious still.

So it is base infidelity to be afraid of our dissolution, when indeed it is not a dissolution, but a way to glory. We should consider the joining rather than the dissolution. Death separates body and soul, but it joins the soul to Christ. It makes the soul more glorious than it was before. We go from glory to glory.

Our Saviour Christ said, 'He that believes in me shall never die' (*John* 11:26). What does he mean by that? Indeed, he shall never die, for grace shall be swallowed up by glory. As soon as the life of nature is gone, he lives the life of glory immediately. So he never dies. There is only an exchange of the life of grace and of nature for the life of glory.

What that glory shall be at that day, it is a part of that glory to know. Indeed, it is beyond the comprehension of our minds. We cannot conceive it; our tongues cannot express it. Peter, as I said, seeing but a glimpse of it, said, 'It is good for us to be here.' He forgot all his former troubles and afflictions. If such a little glimpse of glory could so possess the soul of that blessed man Peter as to make him forget all his former miseries and afflictions, and to be in love with that condition above all others, what shall the glory of heaven be then! Shall we think then of our former misery, and baseness, and trouble, and persecutions? Oh, no.

Use 4. Let us be exhorted by this to test the truth of grace in us, and by our care to proceed from glory to glory, still to be more glorious in Christianity.

We must do this. Let us not deceive ourselves in our natural condition. Are we content to live the life of a sick man? No, we desire health. And when we have health, is that all? No; when we have health we desire strength, too, to encounter oppositions. If that is so in nature, is it not much more so in the new creature, in the new nature, in the divine nature? If there is life, there will be a desire to have health, so that our actions are not sick actions, not weak languishing actions. We desire that God, together with pardoning grace, may join healing grace to cure our souls daily more and more. And then, when we have spiritual health, let us desire spiritual strength to encounter oppositions and temptations, to go through afflictions, to make way through all things that stand in our way to heaven. Let us not deceive ourselves. If there is truth of grace in us, there is still a further desire of grace carrying us to further and further endeavour.

The more we grow in grace, the more God smells a

sweet sacrifice from us. That which comes from us is more refined and less corrupt. It yields better acceptance to God.

The more we grow in grace, the more we grow in ability, in nimbleness, and cheerfulness to do others good. That which comes from us finds more acceptance with others, being carried with a strong spirit of love and delight, which is always accepted in the eyes of men.

And the more we grow in grace, the more cheerful we will be with regard to ourselves. The better we are, the better we may be; the more we do, the more we may do. God instils the oil of grace further, to give us strength and cheerfulness in good actions, so that they come off with delight. Our own cheerfulness increases as our growth increases.

In a word, you see glory tends to glory, and that is enough to stir us up to grow in it. Seeing that glory here, which is grace, tends to glory in heaven, we should never rest till we come to that perfection, till the glory of grace ends in glory indeed. For what is the glory of heaven but the perfection of grace? And what is the beginning of grace here but the beginning of glory? Grace is glory begun, and glory is grace perfected. So if we want to be in heaven as much as may be and enter further and further into the kingdom of God, let us be always adding grace to grace, and one degree to another (*2 Pet.* 1: 5–7).

Objection: But it will be objected that Christians are sometimes at a standstill, and sometimes they seem to go backward.

Answer: Some, because they cannot see themselves growing, think they are not growing at all. That is only ignorance: we see that the sun moves, though we do not see it moving, and we know things grow, though we do not see them growing. So, if we do not perceive our growth from grace to grace, it does not mean we are not growing.

But let's say indeed that Christians decay in their first love and in some grace; there is a suspension of growth. It is that they may grow in some other grace. God sees that they need to grow in the root. So he abases them with some infirmity, and then they spring out in full force again. As after a hard winter comes a glorious spring, so after a setback, grace breaks out more gloriously. There is a mystery in God's method, in that he often increases grace by our sight and sense of our infirmities. God shows his powerful rule in our weakness; God's children never hate their corruption more than when they have been overcome by it. Then they know that there is some hidden corruption that they did not discern before and that they had better take notice of. The best man living does not know himself till he comes to temptation and reveals himself to himself. Temptation uncovers corruption and makes it known, and then stirs up hatred for it. As love stirs up endeavour, so hatred stirs up aversion and loathing. It is profitable for God's children to fall sometimes. Otherwise they would never be as good as they are. They would not wash for the sake of a few spots, but when they see they are foul indeed, they go to wash. But this is a mystery; God wills to have it this way for good ends.

Some good people think they do not have grace because they have only a little. This phrase, 'from glory to glory', shows that we do not have all at once. God carries us from one degree of grace to another. God's children, who have truth of grace in them, have desires that go beyond their endeavour and strength. Their desires are wondrously large, and their prayers correspond to their desires. In the Lord's prayer what do we say? 'Thy kingdom come; thy will be done in earth, as it is in heaven' (*Matt.* 6:10). Can it be so in this world? No. But we must pray till we come to it. We must pray till we come to heaven, where prayer shall cease. So the prayers and desires of God's people transcend their endeavours. Their prayers are infinite.

The chief thing in conversion is the desire, the turning of the stream of the will. So when some Christians find their will and their desire good, but their endeavour to fall short of their purposes, they say, 'Surely I have no good, because I do not have what I want to have'– as if they should have heaven upon earth. But we must grow 'from glory to glory' and thank God for that beginning. It is God's mercy that he would work the least degree of grace in such rebellious hearts as we all have; that he would work any goodness, any change at all. God looks not to the measure as much as to truth. For he will bring truth to perfection, though it might be ever so little. Let us be comforted in this.

And it is God's way to bring his children to glory little by little, so that Christians may depend upon one another, the weaker on the stronger; and so that they may be compassionate and tender toward one another; and so that there may be perpetual experience of God's mercy in helping weak Christians, as well as a perpetual experience of that which is the true ground of comfort: justification. We must be justified and stand righteous before God by Christ's absolute righteousness, having experience of our imperfect righteousness.

So a little measure of grace in us is for great purpose. So let no one be discouraged, especially considering that God, whom we desire to please, values us by that little good we have, and esteems us by that condition of perfection he means to bring us to. As long as we do not yield to our corruptions, but to the Spirit of God, and let him have his work in us, let us be of good comfort in any measure of grace whatsoever.

Use 5. Inasmuch as grace is of a growing nature, in all changes and alterations, whatever we decay in, let us not decay in grace.

Beg of God, 'Lord, whatever thou takest from me, take not thy Spirit from me! Take not thy stamp from me! Let me grow in the inward man although I grow not in the world.' Let us labour to grow 'from glory to glory', though we lose in other ways. What is lost and parted with in the world is well lost if it is for the gain of any grace, because grace is glory. It is a good sickness if it increases patience and humility. It is a good loss if it makes us grow less worldly-minded and more humble. Everything else is vanity in comparison. And that grace that we get by their loss is well gained. Grace is glory; and the more we grow in grace, the more we grow in glory.

Let us then labour to thrive that way, to grow up heavenward, more and more daily. The more grace we get, the more glory. And the more like Christ and God we are, the more we enhance what we profess. And the more we shame Satan and his agencies, and stop their mouths, the more naturally and sweetly duties come from us without constraint. It is good for us to be grown Christians and not be burdened with corruptions. The more we grow, the more active and cheerful and voluntary we will be in duty. We will partake more of that anointing that makes us active in God's service. There is nothing in the world so glorious as a grown Christian. He is compared with the best. If he is a house, he is a temple; if he is a plant, he is a cedar growing up; if he is a flower, he is a lily rising and growing fresher; if he is a stone, he is a pearl. He grows more and more in esteem and use.

If we had spiritual eyes to see the state of a Christian, of a grown Christian especially, we would labour above all things to thrive in this way. Do we not have many works to do? Do we not have many enemies to resist? Do we not have many graces to perfect? Are we not to die and to appear before God? Are we not to enjoy the blessings of God purely? And do not these things require a great deal of strength of grace? Oh, they do. So labour above all things in the world to behold God's love in Christ, and to behold Christ, that by this sight we may grow from glory to glory.

And this will make us willing to die. What makes a man willing to die, but knowing he shall go from glory to greater glory? After death is the perfection of glory. Then we are glorious indeed, when we are in heaven. A weak sight here by faith changes us; but a strong sight, when we shall see face to face, changes us perfectly. Then we shall be like him, when we shall see him face to face.

A wicked man cannot desire death, he cannot desire heaven itself. Why? Because heaven is the perfection of grace. Glory is but grace, which he does not love. So it is proof of future glory when a man loves grace and to grow. I say, such a man is willing to die. A wicked man, who hates grace, who does not love Christ in his image, in his children, or in his truth, hates glory that is the perfection of grace. Grace is the chief part of heaven, the perfection of the image of God, the perfection of all the powers to be like Christ. But as for peace and comfort that spring from it – a wicked man loves peace and quiet, but he does not love to have his nature altered. And if he does not love grace, how can he love glory? No one but a Christian loves heaven. We are ready to drop away daily. It is a fearful thing to be in an unchanged state. Unless we are changed by the Spirit of

God, we shall be afraid to die. We cannot desire to be in heaven. The very heaven of heavens is the perfection of grace. To see God to be all in all, and by the sight of God to be transformed into his likeness, is the chief thing in heaven.

So let us labour more and more to grow in grace, to set Christ before us.

Let me add this one thing: to make use of our examples among us. Christ is now in heaven. But the Spirit of Christ will be in his children to the end of the world, and grace is sweetly conveyed by those that we live among. We grow up in grace by growing in a holy communion with one another. Christ will kindle lights in every generation. Let us labour to have the spirit of those we live with given to us; in daily life, to be like Christ in his members; to love the image of Christ in his children and to associate with them; to be altered into their likeness. This will change us to the glorious likeness of Christ more and more. Those who do not care what company they keep, those who despise the image of Christ in those among whom they live – can they grow in grace?

We shall give account of all the good examples we have had. Does God kindle lights for nothing? We should glorify God for the sun and moon and stars, and other parts of creation. Is not a Christian more glorious than all the creatures in the world? We should glorify God for grace in Christians and labour to be transformed to them, that we may grow more like Christ and more and more glorious. I say this to urge the communion of saints more and more, as we desire to partake more and more of this grace, and to grow 'from glory to glory'.

Use 6. Considering that God means to bring us by degrees to perfect glory of body and soul, and condition in heaven to be like Christ, let this make us content to be humiliated for Christ in this world, *as David, when Michal scorned him, said, 'I will be yet more vile'* (2 Sam. *6:22*).

Let us be content to go out of the camp and bear the reproach of Christ (*Heb.* 13:13). Let the world scorn us for professing religion. God is bringing us from glory to glory, till he brings us to perfect glory; shall we suffer nothing for him? Let us be content to be more contemptible and to bear the reproach of religion. The very worst thing in religion, the reproach of Christ, is better than the treasures of Egypt; Moses made a wise choice (*Heb.* 11:24–26). The very best things in the world are not as good as the worst thing in religion, because reproach ends with assurance that God will take that away and give us glory after. So let us not be dissuaded from a Christian course, but go through both good and bad report, break through all, and finish our course with joy, as St Paul says of himself (*Acts* 20:24).

Use 7. And if it is true that God brings us from glory to glory till he has brought us to perfection of glory, then let us beforehand be thankful to God, *as we see in the epistle of Peter: 'Blessed be the God and Father of our Lord Jesus Christ, that has begotten us to an inheritance incorruptible, undefiled, reserved in heaven'*
(1 Pet. *1:3–4*).

Let us begin the occupation of heaven beforehand. Why does God reveal to us that he will bring us to glory, to that excellent state? That we might begin heaven on earth as much as might be. And how shall we do that? By the occupation of heaven. What is that? 'Holy, holy, holy, Lord God Almighty' (*Rev.* 4:8). There is nothing but magnifying and glorifying God. There shall be no need of prayer. There are praises always; and insofar as we are now praising God and glorifying him for his mercy and love in Christ, we are in heaven before our time. So be stirred up in remembering that we are being led on by degrees, from glory to glory, till we come to perfection. Let us give God the praise for all even beforehand, for it is as sure as if we had it.

It is by faith that things to come are present. Glory to come is present in three ways already, which may stir us up to glorify God beforehand.

The glory to come is present to Christ our head. We, in our husband, are in heaven. Now he has taken heaven for us!

Faith is the evidence of things not seen. It is in the nature of faith to consider future things as present. To faith, future glory is present, present in Christ, and we are part of Christ, Christ mystical, and members. And we in our head are in heaven already, and sit there. And to faith, which makes future things present, we are in heaven already.

And we have the earnest of heaven, the first fruits of the Spirit. We have grace, which is the beginnings of glory. An earnest is never taken away, but the rest is added to complete the bargain. So the earnest of the Spirit of God – the first fruits of peace and joy, of comfort and liberty to the throne of grace – this is the beginning of heaven.

So be praising God continually. Oh, that we could do so! If we could get into a habit of blessing God, we could never be miserable, no, not in the greatest afflictions, for thankfulness has joy always. One who is joyful can never be miserable, for joy enlarges the soul. When is one most joyful, but in a state of thankfulness? And what makes us so thankful as to consider the wonderful things that are reserved in another world, the glory that God is leading us to by steps, from glory to glory, till we are perfect?

'EVEN AS BY THE SPIRIT OF THE LORD'

'As' is understood here according to the phrase in the Greek, and there is a similar word in the Hebrew. Sometimes it signifies likeness and similitude, and sometimes not. It is not here meant as if we were like the Spirit of the Lord, but that this change is brought about even as by the Spirit of the Lord. That is, it is so excellent and so strong that you may know that it is done by none but the Spirit of God.

'As by the Spirit of the Lord' also refers to the degree that the Spirit of the Lord changes us. As there is light no further than the sun shines; so we have no more glory, strength, comfort, peace, or anything gracious or glorious, than the Spirit of God shines into us. It is glorious and excellent, as far as he does it.

So the phrase implies those two things: first, that change is brought by the power of the Spirit, that we may know it is done by the Spirit of the Lord; and then, as by him and no further, for we shine no further than he enlightens us.

You see here the doctrine is clear, that all that I have spoken of before comes from the Spirit of the Lord, and from no other cause. The beholding, the transforming, the degrees of transforming from glory to glory, the taking away of the veil – all is from the Spirit of the Lord. Let us see how this happens.

The Holy Ghost opens our eyes to behold the glory of the Lord, and therefore he is called the Spirit of illumination. The Holy Ghost takes away the veil of ignorance and unbelief and so is called the Spirit of revelation. The Holy Ghost, by revealing the love of God to us in Christ and the love of Christ to us, and by illuminating our understanding to see these things, brings about love to God again, dispensing the love of God to us; and so he is called the Spirit of love. Now when God's love is shed into us by the Spirit of illumination and revelation, we are changed according to the image of Christ. And so the Holy Ghost, from the working of a change, is also called the Spirit of sanctification, because he not only makes us the holy temple of that blessed person, but he makes us holy. And because this change is a glorious change, a change from one degree of grace to another, till we come to be perfect in heaven, he is called a Spirit of glory, as St Peter says, 'the Spirit of glory resteth on you' (*1 Pet.* 4:14), that is, the Spirit of peace, of love, of comfort, of joy. The Spirit, in regard of this blessed attribute, and working all these, is called the Spirit of glory.

The Spirit has various names according to the various operations he works in the saints and people of God. Illumination, revelation, love, sanctification, glory, whatever is worked in man, it is all by the Spirit. Everything comes from the Father as the fountain, and through the Son as mediator; but whatever is worked and brought about is by the Holy Ghost in us, the substantial vigour in the Trinity. All the vigour and operation in the Trinity upon the creature is by the Holy Ghost, the third person. As in the creation the Spirit moved upon the waters, and moving there and brooding on them, fashioned the whole range of the creatures; so the Holy Ghost upon the water of our souls fashions the new creature, brings about all this change 'from glory to glory'. That is why it is here in the passive form, 'We *are changed* from glory to glory, as by the Spirit of the Lord.' So in the chain of salvation our part is passive: 'Whom God foreknew he chose: and whom he chose he justified:

[167]

and whom he justified he glorified' (*Rom.* 8:29–30), all because they come from God and the Spirit of God.

So here we are transformed from glory to glory, all by the Spirit of God, the third person. For, even as all things from God to us come through the Son by the Spirit, so it works back again: all things from us to God must come by the Spirit and through Christ. God gives us the Spirit of prayer and supplication, and the Spirit of sanctification; and we pray in the Spirit, and work in the Spirit, and walk in the Spirit. We do everything in the Spirit, to show that the Spirit does all in all. In this new creature and work of sanctification, it is by no less than the Spirit of the Lord. As it was God who redeemed us, so it is God who must change us. As it was God who brought our salvation and reconciled us – no lesser person could do that – so it is God that must persuade us of that glorious work and fit us for it by his Holy Spirit. It is God who must knit us to our head, Christ, and then little by little transform us to that blessed condition that Christ has purchased for us. God the Son does the one, and God the Spirit does the other.

So we see all the three persons here, for we see the glory of God the Father, the Son, and the Holy Ghost shining in Jesus Christ. Christ is the image according to which we are changed. The Spirit is the one who changes us according to that image. God shows his mercy in Christ. We, knowing and apprehending the mercy of God in Christ by the Spirit, are changed by that Spirit 'from glory to glory'. So the blessed Trinity, as they have a perfect unity in themselves in nature, for they are all one God, have a most perfect unity in their love, care, and respect to mankind. We cannot do without the work of any one of them. Their work is for the good of mankind. The Father in his wisdom decreed and laid the foundation to reconcile mercy and justice in the death of the mediator. Christ brought about our salvation. The Holy Ghost assures us of it and knits us to Christ, and changes and fits us to be members of so glorious a head, and transforms us more and more 'from glory to glory'.

It is comforting to consider how our salvation, and our fitting for salvation till we are put in full possession of it, stand upon the unity of the three glorious persons in the Trinity, and that all join in one to make man happy.

Here, I would like to make two points briefly:

First, the Spirit comes from Christ. It is said here, 'by the Spirit of the Lord', that is, of Christ, because Christ, as well as the Father, breathes (*spirare*). The Father breathes, and so does the Son. The Holy Ghost proceeds by way of spiration from both. So the Spirit is not only the Spirit of the Father, but of the Son, as we see here, 'the Spirit of the Lord'. Christ, as well as the Father, sends the Spirit. 'I will send you the Comforter.' The Holy Ghost proceeds from the Father and the Son, and he relates to us the love of the Father and of the Son. In 2 Corinthians 13:14 we read, 'The grace of our Lord Jesus Christ, the love of God the Father, and the communion of the Holy Ghost.' As the Holy Ghost has communion in proceeding from the Father and the Son and knows the secrets of both, so he reveals them to us. Proceeding from the Son as well as from the Father, he is called here 'the Spirit of the Lord'.

Second, the Spirit is a distinct person from Christ. It is said, 'The Lord is that Spirit.' It might trouble some, how to understand that phrase. Some might think that Christ is all one with the Spirit. But no; here the Spirit is said to be the Spirit of the Lord, meaning he is another distinct person from Christ. The Spirit, as well as

Christ, is God, because the Spirit has the operations of God attributed to him to change, to transform, to make new. We are changed into the same image, from glory to glory, 'even as by the Spirit of the Lord'. Creation and renewal is from an almighty power. All the power of sky and earth could not make something of nothing, or especially of something that is contrary and opposite. For someone opposed to and at enmity with religion to be changed to a better image, to the image of Christ, it takes an almighty power.

I have mentioned these two doctrines in order to come to my main point, which is this:

Whatever is good in us comes from the Spirit of God.

What evidence do I need? Whatever is above nature must come from God's Spirit. The Spirit is the author of all things above nature. Grace, by which we are like Christ, is above nature; therefore it must be by the Spirit of God. Anything that rises from nothing or from something completely opposed, and has Satan to oppose its rising, must be worked by an almighty power. So whoever works anything that is supernaturally good in us must be above the devil. We cannot so much as sincerely confess Jesus Lord but by the Spirit of God. We cannot think a good thought. Everything gracious in us is by the Spirit. I need not belabour so clear a point as this.

USES

Use 1. When you look to have any grace or comfort, then put out of your hearts too much reliance on any outward thing.
Do not think that education or plodding can make us good, or bodily exercise, or listening often to sermons, or conferring often, or taking any pains of our own. Certainly these are things that the Spirit will be effectual

in, if we use them as we should. But without the Spirit what are they? Indeed, what is the body of Christ without the Spirit? 'The flesh profiteth nothing' (*John* 6:63). What is the sacrament and the Word? Dead things without the Spirit of the Lord. Nothing, no outward thing in the world, can work upon the soul but the Spirit of God. And the Spirit of God works upon the soul by the means of grace, altering and changing it according to the image of Christ, more and more.

And in your daily practice do not trust too much in any outward performance or task, making idols of outward things. When people try to improve, they often take great pains in attending sermons, reading, and praying. All these are necessary, but they are dead without the Spirit of Christ. In using all these outward things, whatever they are, look up to Christ, the quickening Spirit, who sends the Spirit into our hearts. The Spirit must give life to all these things, and then something will be accomplished by hearing, and reading, and praying, and receiving the sacrament. In all these look to the Spirit first. We labour in vain if we do not depend wholly upon the Spirit of God and do not trust to a higher strength than our own. It must be a higher strength than our own to work any good in our souls, either grace, or comfort, or peace. And so, as the proverb is, Let the eye be to heaven while the hand is at the helm. Then we shall be transformed and changed by the Spirit of God. Remember that in all means always the Spirit is the principal cause of all. And so before we set upon anything in which we look for spiritual good, desire God by his Holy Spirit that he would give the substance. Words are wind without the Spirit.

The Spirit must go with the ordinances, as the arteries go with the veins. You know that in the body there are arteries. The veins convey the blood, which is a dull thing of itself. But the arteries that come from the heart, the fountain of life, enliven the blood. The Word and truth of God are like the blood in the veins. There is a great deal of matter in them, but there is no life at all. The Spirit must give life to the Word, to clothe those divine truths with the Spirit, and then it works wonders, not otherwise.

Paul spoke to Lydia (*Acts* 16:14) , but the Holy Ghost opened her heart. The Spirit has the key to unlock and open the heart. We speak to the outward man, but unless the inward man is unlocked and opened by the Spirit of God, it is to no purpose. So let us pray for the Spirit of this changing. Everything is by the Spirit of the Lord.

It is so in the mystical Christ even as it was in the natural Christ. All his grace as man was from the Holy Ghost. He was conceived, anointed, sealed and led by the Holy Ghost into the wilderness; he offered himself by the Spirit; he was raised by the Spirit; he was full of the Spirit.

As it was in Christ natural, so it is in Christ mystical; that is, in the church everything is by the Spirit. As he was conceived in the womb by the Spirit, so we are conceived to be Christians by the Spirit. The same Spirit that sanctified him sanctifies us. But first the Spirit sanctifies us by way of union, by knitting us to him the head of all; and then anointing comes after union. The Spirit, when he has knit us to Christ, works the same anointing that he did in Christ. We are called 'Christians', partakers not only of the name, but of the anointing of Christ – that anointing that runs down the head of our spiritual Aaron to the skirts, to every poor Christian. All change, all comfort, all peace is from the Spirit of Christ.

So give him the glory of all. If we find any comfort in any truth, it comes not from us, but from his Spirit, and we must go upward to him again. As all descends from heaven, from the Father of lights and from the Spirit of God, so all must ascend again. Yield him the praise of all. One work of the Spirit is to carry our souls up. For the Spirit, coming from heaven to change, carries us up again to view and to imitate Christ, to be where Christ is. As water when it is to be carried up is carried as high as the spring head from which it came, so the Spirit coming from Christ never stops altering us till we are carried to Christ again. As it is the work of the Spirit to carry us to Christ, then let us desire to be carried beforehand that we may, in thankfulness, begin heaven upon earth. All is from the Spirit of Christ.

A man now in the state of grace must look for nothing from himself. As we are saved altogether outside of ourselves by Christ the mediator, so we are fit for that glorious salvation by the Spirit. Our salvation is worked by God, and the assurance of it is given by the Holy Ghost, by the witness of God sealed to us. We are also prepared, changed and sanctified by the Holy Ghost. Everything is done outside of us in the covenant of grace, in which God is a gracious Father in Christ. Four streams flowed through paradise and watered it, but the head of them was outside of paradise, in another place. In the same way, though the work of the Holy Ghost, the streams of the Spirit, runs through the soul and waters it, the spring of those graces, the Holy Ghost, is outside of us, and Christ the root of salvation is outside of us. He sends his Spirit into us and conveys grace 'from glory to glory' by degrees, and all by the Spirit of the Lord.

Use 2. This thought should comfort us when we find no goodness or strength at all in our natures.
Does God expect us to have anything from ourselves? Who expects anything from a barren wilderness? That is

what our hearts are like, and God knows it well enough. There is no goodness in us, no more than there is moisture in a stone or a rock. He looks for us to beg the Spirit of him, and depend upon him for the Spirit of his Son to open our eyes with the Spirit of illumination, to reveal his love to us, and then to sanctify us, to work out all corruption little by little, and to work us more and more to glory. He expects us to depend on him for the Spirit in all we do.

Christians, therefore, are much to blame. They try to work and to hew out of their own nature the love of God and keep going by their own efforts, as if they had a principle of grace in themselves. And they may work that way for a long time. But that is not the way. Instead we must acknowledge that in and of ourselves, as St Paul says, we cannot do anything (*Phil.* 2:13). We cannot so much, by all the power in the world, as think a good thought. If we should live a thousand years, there cannot rise out of our hearts, of ourselves, a good desire. It is all from outside of ourselves, from the Spirit of the Lord.

We must not look for it in ourselves, but go to God for his Holy Spirit. Go to Christ for his Spirit, that he would enlighten us and sanctify us. We must not presume that we can do anything of ourselves.

And so we must not despair. Shall we despair when once we believe in Christ, when we have abundance of grace and Spirit in our head, Christ? And he can convey his Spirit as he pleases. He gives the Spirit by degrees as he pleases, for he is a voluntary head to dispense it as he will. He is not a natural head. Who shall despair when he is in Christ, who is complete? And in him we receive grace for grace, grace corresponding to grace in him.

Let no one presume that he can do anything of himself, for you see how God allowed holy men to fail miserably. It was folly in Peter to presume of his own strength that though all might forsake Christ, yet he would not (*Mark* 14:29,31). God left him to himself, and you see how he fell. So it is with us all, when we presume upon the strength of our own nature and abilities.

We must not come to this holy place in our own strength, but with a desire that the Spirit may join with his ordinances and make them efficacious for our change. All change is by the Spirit of the Lord. Nothing works above its own sphere. It is above the power of nature to work anything supernatural. If we wish to profit by the Word, we must not come with presumptuous spirits, but lift up our hearts to God, that his Spirit may give life and power to the ministry, that he may convey holy truths into our hearts to change the inward and the outward man. Then we come as we should. Everything is done by the Spirit of the Lord, blessing all means, and without whom all means are dead.

We must open as a flower that opens when the sun shines on it. We open as Christ shines on us, and ebb and flow as he flows upon us. As things around us are light only when the sun shines, so we are light and open and flow and are carried to anything only when Christ by his Spirit flows on us. We do what we do, but we first receive power from the Spirit. We listen and do good works, but the activity and power and strength all come from the Spirit of God.

Use 3. We may test ourselves in several ways to see whether we have the Spirit of Christ or not. I will not go out of the text for this.

If a man has the Spirit of God, the eyes of the soul are open to see in the glass of the Word the face of God

[175]

shining on him in Christ. If a man has the Spirit, he sees God as a Father by the Spirit of illumination.

If we have the Spirit of God, we have the Spirit of love. God's Spirit manifests to our soul the hidden love of God, for the Spirit of God searches the secret of God, and searches our heart. He that has the Spirit of God knows the love of God in Christ to him; its height, and breadth, and depth are revealed to our spirits. As in the text, we see the gracious love of God in Christ, and then we love him in return.

Where the Spirit is, it changes us. It is a Spirit not only of illumination, but of sanctification. Where he dwells he sanctifies the house and makes it a temple. Where the Spirit is, it will work. It is like the wind: where it is, it will stir and move things, and if things are not moved, it is not there. If the condition is not altered from bad to good, and from good to better, suspect that the Spirit is not there. There will always be some discernible operation of the Spirit of God.

Some slander us, saying that we think to 'put on Christ's righteousness' but are not changed a whit. But we teach that the Spirit of God first opens our eyes. Then he takes off the veil, and we see the glory of God's mercy in Christ, pardoning our sins for the righteousness and obedience of Christ. And that love warms our hearts, so that it changes our hearts by the Spirit, from one degree of grace to another. There is a changing power that goes with the love of Christ and with the mercy of God in Christ. This is our doctrine. The same Spirit that justifies us by applying to us the obedience of Christ also sanctifies us. So their allegations are unfounded; we see here that the Spirit of the Lord does change us.

And there are those who profess themselves Christians, who partake of the name, but not of the anointing of Christ. In true Christians, the anointing with the Spirit of Christ will force a change. We cannot behold the sun without taking in some light; and we cannot behold the Sun of righteousness without being changed and enlightened. A man may look up at the sky for other reasons, but still at the same time he will have the sun's light cast on him. And when with the eye of faith we look upon Christ for justification and forgiveness of sins, at the same time imperceptibly there is an alteration of the soul, though we are not thinking about it. At the very instant that we apprehend justification and forgiveness of sins in the mercy of God in Christ, there is a glory put upon the soul. We cannot deal with the God of glory without being glorious. There is no one that has anything to do with God, who does not have some glory put into his soul.

So let no one think he is a Christian who does not find the work of the Spirit altering him. The Spirit has the title of Holy Spirit, from the blessed work of sanctifying and changing: he changes us.

And when he has changed us, he governs and guides us from glory to glory. Where the Holy Ghost is, he advances the work of grace that has begun. Those who have the Spirit of God do not rest in one degree of grace, but grow from grace to grace, from knowledge to knowledge, from faith to faith, till they come to that measure of perfection that God has appointed them in Christ. Those who will go no further and think all is well do not have the Spirit of God. For the Spirit stirs us up to grow from one degree of grace to another, to add grace to grace, and to enter further and further into the kingdom of grace, and to come nearer still to glory.

To this end the Holy Spirit dwells in us and guides us (*Rom.* 8:26). He is a tutor to us. Where the Holy Ghost is in anyone, it is as a counsellor. 'Guide me with thy

[177]

counsel, and afterward receive me to glory' (*Psa.* 73:24). It is as a tutor. Noblemen's children have their tutors, and God's children are nobly born. They have their tutor and counsellor, as well as angels to attend them. They have the Spirit of God to tell them, 'Do this, and do that, and there you have done wrong.' They have a voice behind them to teach them in particular how they have gone astray. Those who have the Spirit find a sweet operation of the Spirit as teacher and counsellor. Those acquainted with the governing of God's Spirit find it checking them immediately when they do wrong. It grieves them when they grieve the Spirit. So it teaches them in specific situations, 'Do this, do not do that.'

In this way, then, we may know if we have the Spirit, if it guides and governs us from glory to glory, till we come to perfection, where the Spirit is all in all in heaven.

Another evidence is this: the Spirit, where present, rests and abides, because it not only changes us at first, but continues leading us from glory to glory. As St Augustine said, 'Wicked men have the Spirit of God knocking, and he would fain enter.' When the wickedest man hears holy truths revealed, he finds sweet stirrings in his poisonous, rebellious nature as the Spirit of God knocks at his heart. Here the Spirit is knocking to have entrance. But God's children have the Spirit entering, dwelling and resting there. The Spirit of God rests on Christ and on Christ's members. How can he change them and, having done so, guide and govern them from glory to glory, unless he rests there and takes up lodging and residence? A Christian is not an ordinary house, but a temple; he is not an ordinary man, but a king; he is not an ordinary stone, but a pearl; he is not an ordinary tree, but a cedar; he is an excellent person. And therefore the Spirit of God delights to dwell in him. As the excellency of the body comes from the soul, so the excellency of the soul comes from the Spirit dwelling in him. However, when at times the Spirit suspends his acts of comforting and guiding, to humble us for our presumption, always the Holy Ghost is in the heart, though hidden in a corner of the heart. 'The Comforter shall abide with you for ever,' said Christ (*John* 14:16).

And so we see how we may test ourselves as to whether or not we have the Spirit of the Lord. If we do not have the Spirit, we are none of his, we are none of Christ's (*Rom.* 8:9).

But then, whose are we if we are none of Christ's? Do think of that. If we do not want to be without the Spirit, that is, dead men, led by a spirit worse than our own, let us labour to know whether or not we have the Spirit of Christ. Let us see what change there is to the likeness of Christ.

The Spirit, who comes from the Lord, makes us like the Lord; and we are changed by what comes from Christ and from the love of God in Christ, because whatever the Spirit has he takes from Christ (*John* 16:13–15). He comforts the soul with the love of God in Christ, shown through his death and shed blood. God has given his Son, and Christ has given himself, and we feel the love of God by the Spirit.

If the Spirit works any grace or comfort by what comes from Christ, this is the true Spirit. The change worked in us is according to the image of Christ, that we may be like him. So Christ is the beginning and the end, and Christ is all. The Spirit works from Christ and to him. Let us examine whether we have the Spirit of Christ by whether it changes us, and then, if we have the Spirit, examine by what reasons and grounds it changes us. Then we may say we have the Spirit.

Use 4. If we do not have the Spirit, how shall we come to have the Spirit?

This chapter sets out that excellently.

First, *the gospel is called the ministry of the Spirit,* for the opening of the love of God in Christ, which is the gospel, is the ministry of the Spirit. Why? Because God has joined the Spirit with making these mysteries known. Then study the gospel, and hear divine truths unfolded. The more we hear of the sweet love of God in Christ, the more the Spirit flows with it into the soul. Let us delight in hearing spiritual truth, the love of God made known in Christ.

A civil moral man is in his element and is greatly stirred when he hears a moral, witty political speech. And this has its use. But what is that to the gospel? The Spirit goes with the unfolding of the gospel; and if our hearts are ever seasoned with the love of God, these teachings about Christ and the benefits and privileges by Christ will affect us more than anything else in the world.

That is one means: to study the gospel, and to hear the truths of the gospel opened where the Spirit works.

The Spirit of the Lord is given to us usually in holy community. The Holy Ghost fell upon them in the Acts when they were gathered together (*Acts* 4:31). And surely we never find sweeter stirrings of the Spirit than when we are gathered at such times about holy business. We never find the Spirit more effectual to change our souls than at those times. 'Where two or three are gathered together, I will be in the midst of you,' said Christ (*Matt.* 18:20), but by the Spirit, warming and changing the soul. God infuses all grace in communion, as we are members of the body mystical. Those with sullen spirits, a spirit of separation, who scorn all meetings, are carried with the spirit of the devil and of the world. They do not know what belongs to the things of God. It is the meek spirit that subjects itself to the ordinance of God. The Holy Ghost falls upon men usually when they are in holy communion.

God will give the Holy Ghost to all who beg him (*Luke* 11:13). Pray for the Holy Ghost as the most excellent thing in the world. He shall be given to those who beg him as if to say there is nothing greater than that. Come to God, and in anything we have to do, let us empty ourselves and beg the Spirit. The more we empty ourselves of our own confidence in regard of performance of holy duties, the more we will desire to be filled with the fullness of the Spirit. This sense of our own emptiness will compel prayer.

We must remember that of ourselves we can do nothing in a holy and acceptable way, except by the Spirit. So let us do everything with a sense of our own emptiness, and beg the Spirit.

It is the same when the Spirit grants us the will to obey. The Spirit joins more and more closely with the souls of those who obey his stirrings. God gives his Spirit to those who obey him. Those who obey the first stirrings of the Spirit find that they have the Spirit to a fuller degree.

Why do people have no more Spirit in the ordinances? The Holy Ghost knocks at their hearts and would willingly enter, but they resist, as Stephen says (*Acts* 7:51). If we want to have him more and more, let us open our souls that the king of glory may come in. The Spirit is willing to enter, especially in holy assemblies. 'I was in the Spirit on the Lord's day,' says St John (*Rev.* 1:10); that is, as if he were drowned in the Spirit on the Lord's day. We are never more in the Spirit than when we are about holy exercises.

[181]

Let us open our souls to the Spirit, and then we shall find the Spirit joining with our souls. The Spirit is more willing to save us and to sanctify us than we are to entertain him. Oh, that we were willing to entertain the sweet stirrings of the Spirit! Our natures would not be so defiled, and we would not lack so in comfort as we do. There is not one of us who does not find comforting stirrings in holy exercises. That is how we may get the Spirit of the Lord, who does all, illuminates, sanctifies, rules and rests in us.

Use 5. And let us learn to give the third glorious person, the Holy Ghost, his due.
Since we have everything by the Spirit, let us learn to give the Spirit his due and learn how to make use of the work of the Spirit.

There are several works of the Spirit. We see in this text by the phrase 'we all' what the Spirit does: the Spirit unites us. It is a Spirit of union, knitting all together by one faith to God. All meet in God the Father reconciled; and we all are joined together by love, by the Spirit, 'with open face'.

Who takes away the veil? We are all veiled by nature. The Spirit takes away the veil from our eyes, and from the truth. Why is the gospel so obscure? Either the Spirit does not take away the veil, does not teach by the ministry; or else it does not take away the veil from the eyes. The Spirit takes away the scales from our eyes, and the Spirit in the ministry takes away the obscurity of the Scriptures. All those that we call graces, the free gifts, the ministerial gifts, are the gifts and graces of the Spirit, and they are for the graces of the Spirit. Skill in languages, in the Scriptures and in other learning, are given to men so that they may take away the veil from the Scriptures, that they may give light. And when the

Spirit is given, he takes away the veil from the soul by his own work.

And then with open face 'we behold the glory of the Lord'. What opens our eyes to see, when the veil is taken off? The Spirit. We have no inward light or sight, except by the illumination of the Spirit. All light in the things and all sight we have is by the illumination of the Spirit.

And the change according to the image of Christ is altogether by the Spirit of Christ, altogether from the Holy Ghost. Christ baptizes 'with the Holy Ghost, and with fire' (*Matt.* 3:11), and Christ came 'by water and blood' (*1 John* 5:6): by blood, to die for us; and by water, by his Spirit, to change and purge and cleanse us. All is by the Spirit. Christ came as well by the Spirit as by blood. This change, and the gradual change from glory to glory, all is by the Spirit. So we should think not only of Christ, or of God the Father when we go to God in prayer, but of the work of the Spirit, that the Holy Ghost may have his due.

Lord, without thy Spirit, my body is like a dead, stiff corpse that cannot stir; and my soul, too, without the operation of thy Holy Spirit, is stiff, dead and unmoveable. By thy Spirit, breathe upon me, as thy Holy Spirit in the creation lay upon the waters and fashioned heaven and earth. The Spirit of God lying upon the waters of the soul fashions all graces and comforts in the new creature, just as all in this glorious fabric of the world was made by the Spirit of God. Let the Spirit of God, then, have due acknowledgement in all things whatever.

And what are we to look to mainly now? The knowledge of God the Father and his love to us shining in Christ. All is in Christ. And if we want to have have any alteration of our natures, let us beg the Spirit, that we may know the love of God in Christ and the Spirit attending upon the gospel.

And because we have all these abundantly in these latter times of the church, in the reformation of religion, there is a second spring of the gospel. Never since the beginning of the world have there been such glorious times as we enjoy. We see how the holy apostle prefers these times over former times, when the veil was upon their eyes and all was hidden in ceremonies and types and such things among the Jews. 'Now', he says, 'we behold the glory of God, and are changed by the Spirit from glory to glory.'

7: *Conclusion*

Consider that the glory of the times, and the glory of places and persons, is all from the revelation of Christ by the Spirit. The more God in Christ is laid open, the more the times, places, and persons are excellent. What made the second temple superior to the former? Christ came at the second temple. Though baser in itself, the second temple was more glorious than the first. What made Bethlehem, that little city, glorious? Christ was born there. What makes the heart where Christ is born more glorious than in other folks? Christ is born there. Christ makes persons and places glorious. What makes the times now more glorious than they were before Christ? What made the least in the kingdom of heaven greater than John the Baptist? He was greater than all that were before him; and all that are after him are greater than he. Because his head was cut off, he did not see the death and resurrection of Christ and the giving of the Holy Ghost. He did not see so much of Christ. So it is the revelation of Christ and the love of God in Christ that makes times and persons and places glorious, all glorious, because the veil is taken away from our eyes. We see Christ the king of glory in the gospel flourishing and the love of God manifested, and by the Spirit of God the veil is taken away inwardly as well as outwardly.

The glory of these present times comes from a fuller revelation of Christ than in former times. Now there are more converted than in former times, because the Spirit goes together with the manifestation of Christ. Why is this kingdom more glorious than any place beyond the seas? Because Christ is here revealed more fully than there. The veil is taken off, and here 'we see the glory of God with open face', which changes many thousands from glory to glory by the Spirit of God that accompanies the revelation of the gospel. Is there any outward thing that advances our kingdom above Turkey or Spain or others? No, nothing. They have as much as we do, if not more, in the way of government and riches and outward things. But the glory of places and times is from the revelation of Christ, which has the Spirit accompanying it. That Spirit changes us 'from glory to glory'. Our times are more glorious than they were a century or two ago. Why? Because we see Christ revealed, and the gospel opened, and the veil taken off.

Now this revelation challenges us to acknowledge these blessed times. What should all this do but stir us up to know the time of our visitation, and to bless God, who has reserved us for these places and countries and for this time of glorious gospel light. Now we live under the gospel, by which 'with open face' we see the glory of the mercy of God in Christ, the 'unsearchable riches' of Christ opened to us. And together with the gospel, the ministry of the Spirit, goes the Spirit. And those thousands that belong to God are being changed by the blessing of God from glory to glory.

Certainly if we share in the good of the times we will have hearts to thank God and to walk in ways corresponding to it; that as we have the glorious gospel, we will walk gloriously and not dishonour so glorious a gospel by base and fruitless lives. Let us remember the times: if we are no better for these glorious times, if the veil is not taken away, we are under a fearful judgement.

'The god of this world hath blinded our eyes' (*2 Cor.* 4:4).

Do we live under the glorious light and yet are dark and see no glory in Christ? Is this the fruit of the long preaching of the gospel, and the veil being taken off so long? Certainly the god of this world has cast the dust of the world into our eyes, so that we can see nothing but earthly things. We are under the seal of God's judgement. He has sealed us up to a dark state, from darkness of judgement to the darkness of hell without repentance. Let us beware of living in a dull and dead condition, under the glorious gospel, or else how cursed we shall be! The more we are exalted and lifted up above other people in the blessings of God this way, the more we shall be cast down. 'Woe unto thee, Chorazin' (*Matt.* 11:21). 'How shall we escape if we neglect so great salvation?' (*Heb.* 2:3).

Let us take heed not to while away our time, these precious times and blessed opportunities. If we do not labour to get out of the state of nature into the state of grace, and so to be changed from glory to glory, God in justice will curse the means we have, that in hearing we shall not hear, and seeing we shall not see, and he will secretly and imperceptibly harden our hearts. It is the curse of all curses to grow worse and duller when we have so much opportunity.

Let us labour for hearts that know the mercies of God in Christ, and labour to be transformed and moulded into this gospel every day more and more.

ANALYSIS

fication, we are liberated from slavery to sin
and are freed to do good; questions of effectual grace and liberty answered; in final glory
we shall be perfectly freed

Liberty of the gospel

The liberty of the church, of the Word and
sacraments, brings and preserves spiritual
liberty

USES

1. All liberties are by the Spirit; let us labour to
have the Spirit
2. Comfort in all conditions: temptation, sickness,
death
3. Knowing whether we are at liberty: by holiness; a
full heart; courage; boldness with God; freedom
from the errors of the times
4. Take heed not to grieve the Spirit

4: *The gospel is beyond the law*

*'But we all, as in a glass, with open face behold the glory
of the Lord, and are changed into the same image,
from glory to glory, as by the Spirit of the Lord.'*
A brief comparison of the administration of the
covenant of grace with that of the law

5: *Our communion and fellowship with God in Christ*

The grace and free mercy of God are his glory,
especially his mercy shining in Jesus Christ

'The glory of the Lord'

USES

1. Let us justify God and his plan by embracing
Christ

2. Christ has no partner in salvation

3. Let us remember the gloriousness of God's mercy in Jesus Christ

'As in a glass'

We see God in Christ and in the gospel, the Word; these are 'glasses'

Why we must see 'in a glass' and not directly

'We behold'

Spiritual sight compared to physical sight; knowledge and faith compared to sight

Making the eye of our souls fit to behold the glory of God

'With open face'

To behold the glory of God, a double veil is taken away: the veil of obscurity and the veil of slavery

'We all'

All, Jews and Gentiles, may have grace; Christ's body, the church, is a communion

6: *Our conformity to the image of Christ*

'And are changed'

The necessity of being changed: to be made fit for communion with God and for heaven; for power against sin; for a change in the will to make holy actions possible; to qualify us for glory

'Into the same image'

How and why we are changed into the image of Christ, the second Adam

USES

1. Let us study and behold Christ more, that we may be like him; we are planted into the likeness

of his death and resurrection; knowing if the image of Christ is stamped upon us

2. Let us fix our meditations upon him

3. Let us look at our own corruptions and go to Christ; Christ, being made man, was once conformed to us; we have the Spirit, who does all; we are changed both by power and by reason; whatever is good in us, see it first in Christ

4. Three sights are the foundation of all comfort: God sees us in Christ; Christ sees us in his Father's love; we see Christ and ourselves in Christ, and the love of God to us in Christ

'From glory to glory' (1)

Glory here means especially grace and the favour of God

The glory of a Christian: conversion, growth in assurance; the presence of God in heaven; the day of judgement

Grace is glory, and grace is growing; so we grow 'from glory to glory'

Why the world despises those who have grace

USES

1. If grace is glory, let us labour for grace above all things

2. Set God's judgement against the world's scorn

3. How we should regard ourselves

4. Take comfort in the work of grace, though so disparaged by the world

5. Knowing whether we have grace in us

'From glory to glory' (2)

The state of believers both here and in heaven is called glory; the difference is one of degree

The more grace grows, the more it shines; and
there must be an increase

USES
1. Labour to have more and more grace
2. Do not be discouraged
3. Do not be afraid of death, for grace will end in
   glory
4. Test the truth of grace in ourselves and proceed
   from glory to glory; why Christians sometimes
   seem at a standstill
5. Do not decay in grace
6. Be content to be humiliated for Christ in this
   world
7. Be thankful to God beforehand; glory to come is
   present in some ways already

'*Even as by the Spirit of the Lord*'
Change is brought about by the power of the Spirit
and from no other cause
Whatever is good in us comes from the Spirit of
God

USES
1. Do not rely on outward things for grace or
   comfort
2. The thought that all is done by the Spirit should
   comfort us when we find no strength or goodness in ourselves
3. Testing ourselves to see whether we have the
   Spirit of Christ: the eyes of the soul are opened;
   we have the Spirit of love; he changes us; he
   governs and guides; he dwells in us and is a
   tutor; he continues leading; he makes us like the
   Lord

[193]

4. To have the Spirit: study and hear gospel truth;
   be in holy community; ask God
5. Let us give the Holy Ghost his due

7: *Conclusion*

A challenge to make the most of these blessed times in
which Christ is revealed more fully

SOME OTHER
BANNER OF TRUTH
TITLES

THE BRUISED REED

Richard Sibbes

In his famous exposition of Isaiah 42:3 and Matthew 12:20, Sibbes (1577–1635) unfolds the tender ministry of Jesus Christ, who is 'a physician good at all diseases, especially at the binding up of the broken heart'. This work has been of spiritual help and comfort to a very wide range of readers, including Richard Baxter in the seventeenth century and Dr Martyn Lloyd-Jones in the twentieth. 'What insights into the unexpected ways in which a Christian triumphs! Perhaps most surprising [is] the aptness of his observations concerning the state of the church, as if this book were written yesterday!' (*Evangelical Times*).

ISBN: 0 85151 740 4
138 pp. Paperback
£2.50/$4.99

The PURITAN PAPERBACKS series:

A Lifting Up for the Downcast, William Bridge
ISBN 0 85151 298 4, 288 pp.
The Mystery of Providence, John Flavel
ISBN 0 85151 104 X, 224 pp.
Prayer, John Bunyan
ISBN 0 85151 090 6, 176 pp.
Precious Remedies Against Satan's Devices,
Thomas Brooks,
ISBN 0 85151 002 7, 256 pp.
The Rare Jewel of Christian Contentment,
Jeremiah Burroughs
ISBN 0 85151 091 4, 232 pp.
The Reformed Pastor, Richard Baxter
ISBN 0 85151 191 0, 256 pp.
The Shorter Catechism Explained from Scripture,
Thomas Vincent
ISBN 0 85151 314 X, 280 pp.
The Sinfulness of Sin, Ralph Venning
ISBN 0 85151 647 5, 284 pp.
A Sure Guide to Heaven, Joseph Alleine
ISBN 0 85151 081 7, 148 pp.
The True Bounds of Christian Freedom,
Samuel Bolton
ISBN 0 85151 083 3, 224 pp.

For free illustrated catalogue please write to
THE BANNER OF TRUTH TRUST
3 Murrayfield Road, Edinburgh EH12 6EL, UK
P O Box 621, Carlisle, Pennsylvania 17013, USA